# THE
# WONDERS
# WE
# SEEK

# THE WONDERS WE SEEK

## Thirty Incredible Muslims Who Helped Shape the World

by Saadia Faruqi and Aneesa Mumtaz

illustrated by Saffa Khan

Quill Tree Books
An Imprint of HarperCollins Publishers

Quill Tree Books is an imprint of HarperCollins Publishers.

The Wonders We Seek: Thirty Incredible Muslims Who Helped Shape the World

Library of Congress Cataloging-in-Publication Data
[TK]
ISBN 978-0-06-297344-3

Typography by Erin Fitzsimmons
22 23 24 25 26  RTLO  10 9 8 7 6 5 4 3 2 1

First Edition

## Dear Reader,

If you're reading this book, it means you're interested in the origins of the sciences and arts. It means you're open to hearing new ideas, even if they clash with what you may already believe. That's good. That means you're ready to learn.

We wrote this book because we want everyone to know about the amazing contributions of Muslims throughout history, all the way up to the present. These days, the news you see on television and read on the internet may make you believe that Muslims are backward, and that the countries we live in are devoid of science or technology. That all the brave and smart and powerful people live in the Western world. We wrote this book to shed light on people and events that tell us different. We wrote this book to uncover the accomplishments of Muslims that will leave you awed and inspired. Finally, we want our Muslim readers to feel pride and joy in this heritage.

The most important fact to remember is that many of the inventions we see today, much of learning and discovery, happened centuries ago through the effort and hard work of ancient people in medieval kingdoms and faraway lands. But if you think that was Europe during the sixteenth, seventeenth, and eighteenth centuries, you'd be wrong. Think further back, to the seventh to tenth centuries. Consider the lands of Arabia, Iraq, Persia, and India. Hundreds of years before Europeans even knew that washing hands was an essential part of hygiene, Muslims in the Arab world were devising medical equipment that is still used in hospitals today. A thousand years before the Wright brothers, Arabs and Persians were creating flying machines and attempting to emulate birds. Female warriors and rulers were flourishing. Art, music, astronomy, physics, mathematics, and so many other fields of knowledge were being shared and created and discussed by Muslims a very, very long time ago. This tradition of learning, dedication, and progress continues in all corners of the globe, from Pakistan and Bangladesh to Egypt and Indonesia and even China.

Why? Human creativity, curiosity, and ingenuity definitely play a role. But a big reason is that discovery and learning are part of the Islamic faith. Muslims are commanded in our holy book, the Quran, to seek knowledge and study nature for signs of the Almighty. The earliest Muslims used books of ancient Greek learning and continued their quest for knowledge. Everything they discovered and understood was written and translated over time into Latin, French, German, and English, until it fueled Europe's Renaissance and the scientific revolution.

But this book is more than just a history book. It includes personalities who lived hundreds of years ago, as well as those who are currently alive. It showcases achievements in so many different areas, including music, medicine, politics, human rights, literature, sports, technology, and more. Our goal is to bring to light Muslims who have made a tremendous, lasting difference in the world, and hence in all of us.

This was no easy task, we assure you. Compiling this book was challenging. We and our research assistant, Rich Heffron, worked hard to sift through countless personalities. Who do we choose to include, what criteria do we utilize, and how do we decide who to leave out? We wanted to include all the brightest geniuses of the ancient world and all the incredibly hardworking, selfless people of modern times. Yet we were limited by many factors.

First of all, we don't have sufficient biographical information about many Muslims who lived centuries ago. Take the example of al-Khwarizmi, the father of algebra and algorithms. He was a treasure for the entire world in the ways that he built the basics of modern applied mathematics and created the first algorithm. If you grow up to be physicists or mathematicians or work in space exploration or computer technology, you'll see how important his contributions are. But we couldn't include him in this book because we have almost no information about him as a person. Nothing about his early life or his family. What we have are the books he wrote and the work he left behind.

Therefore, we had to create strict criteria during our research process. To be included in this book:

- the person must claim to be Muslim as far as we know, *and*
- the person must have broken a barrier, that is, been the first or the best at something, *or*
- the person must have made some major contribution that affected positively the world at large.

This meant, unfortunately, that a lot of people who are amazing personal heroes of ours didn't make the cut. For example, Abdul Sattar Edhi from Pakistan and Hawa Abdi from Somalia were extraordinary but didn't have an impact outside their own countries. It also meant that some people who weren't the most selfless human beings got included in the list, such as Benazir Bhutto, the first female leader of a modern Islamic country. Thirdly, it meant that unless we could have a pretty strong idea that someone was a Muslim in terms of their own stated beliefs, we wouldn't be able to highlight their achievements.

Finally, a caveat. This book is not the ultimate sourcebook for Muslim achievement. Our hope in writing it is to merely offer a starting point for discussions and further study. Once you read about ancient Baghdad and Spain, it should whet your appetite to know more. It should propel you to do further research and dig into the details of our shared history on this planet. Once you read about the role models we have today and the amazing challenges they faced in their tasks, hopefully it will lead to your own goals and inspiration.

So, go ahead and read about some of the most remarkable human beings on planet earth. We hope you'll be as inspired and motivated as we were while writing about them.

Happy reading,
Saadia Faruqi and Aneesa Mumtaz

# CONTENTS

Al-Ma'mun                          XX

Al-Zahrawi                         XX

Ibn al-Haytham                     XX

Ibn Sina                           XX

Saladin                            XX

Razia Sultan                       XX

Jalal al-Din Rumi                  XX

Ibn Battuta                        XX

Zheng He                           XX

Abdul Rahman                       XX

Nana Asma'u                        XX

Naguib Mahfouz                     XX

Noor Inayat Khan                   XX

Malcolm X                          XX

Mohammad Abdus Salam               XX

Fazlur Rahman Khan                 XX

Ayub Khan Ommaya            XX

Farouk El-Baz               XX

Fatima Mernissi             XX

Muhammad Yunus              XX

Muhammad Ali                XXX

Rebiya Kadeer               XXX

Kareem Abdul-Jabbar         XXX

Shirin Ebadi                XXX

Yusuf Islam/Cat Stevens     XXX

Benazir Bhutto              XXX

Rana Dajani                 XXX

Sharmeen Obaid-Chinoy       XXX

Ibtihaj Muhammad            XXX

Malala Yusufzai             XXX

Glossary                    XXX

Sources                     XXX

# AL-MA'MUN

## PATRON OF BIG SCIENCE

*While Europe was struggling with superstition and ignorance in the Dark Ages, the Islamic empire was preparing for its Golden Age. The Abbasid caliphate was one of the largest and most well known in the empire, having control of key regions from the years 750 to 1258. Abdullah al-Rashid, known as Caliph al-Ma'mun, was the seventh ruler of the caliphate.*

### A Lucky Birth

Al-Ma'mun was born in the newly created city of Baghdad in 786. This was the same year his father, Harun al-Rashid, made famous by the stories in *The Thousand and One Nights*, came to power. Al-Ma'mun would often be seen playing with his father in the palace gardens on the banks of the Tigris River. He grew up during the height of the glory days of Baghdad, already the largest city in the world. In just forty years, Baghdad had surpassed every other ancient city—Rome, Athens, or Alexandria—in terms of size and grandeur. From palaces to markets, and with multistory buildings as tall as nine floors high, Baghdad was the center of the peak of technology in ancient times.

## From Scholar to Warrior

As a young man, al-Ma'mun studied religious texts as well as poetry and Arabic grammar, along with mathematics. He was a brilliant student and a very quick study. His personal tutor was Ja'far, a Persian minister in his father's court. Ja'far was responsible for instilling a love for learning that would guide al-Ma'mun throughout his life. He was also exposed to a wide variety of ideas and cultures through the melting pot that Baghdad had become. From Greek to Persian, and from Indian to Chinese, he was exposed to all traditions and knowledge.

Harun al-Rashid died in 809, leaving al-Ma'mun's younger half-brother, al-Amin, as his heir. Al-Ma'mun was given Khorasan, an ancient region now in Turkmenistan, as a consolation prize. This led to a bloody feud between the two brothers. Their armies fought battles in other areas such as modern-day Tehran, culminating in a terrible siege of Baghdad in 812. After more than a year, al-Amin's forces surrendered, but not before they destroyed the beautiful city their ancestors had built. Al-Amin was killed, and al-Ma'mun went back to Khorasan as caliph.

## A Thirst for Knowledge

Al-Ma'mun was by no means a popular ruler. Many people considered him a usurper, while others did not like his support of the Shia Muslims, a minority branch of Islam. He could be cruel and unyielding in political matters. After only a few years, rebellions started against him, and he decided to return to Baghdad once and for all. There he began to put his dream into action: the promotion of ideas from around the world. Translation of Greek and Persian works had already begun under earlier caliphs, and his father had already begun a majestic library, but al-Ma'mun wanted to go further. He wanted all the knowledge of the world at his fingertips.

During his reign, al-Ma'mun created an environment that encouraged discovery, invention, debate, and curiosity. He not only encouraged his own Muslim subjects to study, but also invited people from other faiths and regions to settle in Baghdad. He employed scholars in all fields, who wanted to study and improve upon the knowledge already at their disposal. He financially supported numerous endeavors to translate books into Arabic, so that his scholars would be able to learn from them and further their fields. Under his patronage, Arabic scholarship grew tremendously, with original writings in subjects like astronomy, medicine, geography, and mathematics.

## An Environment of Learning

Al-Ma'mun instituted a number of policies and practices to encourage an environment of learning. He started weekly sessions of debate and discussion at his court, at which anyone with good ideas would feel free to present them directly to the caliph. He sent emissaries to far-off lands in search of books, and often accepted as ransom books rather than gold from prisoners of war. He established an impressive academy called the House of Wisdom, which became the center of all his scholarly activities, and expanded his father's collection of books and manuscripts. There, teams of scholars from all faiths were employed to study, write about, and further every aspect of the sciences. Great personalities such as al-Khwarizmi, the father of algebra, and al-Kindi, the father of Arab philosophy, worked there.

Al-Ma'mun was not satisfied with establishing the House of Wisdom for study alone. He wanted to create new inventions, discover new parts of the world and the skies. To learn more about the universe, he commissioned the building of two observatories. His astronomers created astronomical tables and calculations of the stars, sun, and moon, like the world had never seen before. His scientists calculated accurately the circumference of the earth. And finally, his geographers undertook the task of making a map of the entire known world. This ambitious project was completed in 833, the year of al-Ma'mun's death, and included inhabited and barren regions, settlements, and cities.

### An Ending and a Beginning

Caliph al-Ma'mun died unexpectedly in 833 at only forty-seven years of age. Despite his loss as a funder of the sciences, the House of Wisdom continued under subsequent caliphs. Baghdad continued to provide support to scholars and fuel the Golden Age. In 1258, with the invasion of Mongol armies, the House of Wisdom, along with much of Baghdad, was destroyed.

Despite his political harshness, al-Ma'mun remains the first and only true patron of the sciences in the Golden Age of Islam. Without his financial support and political encouragement, many of the brilliant minds of that time may not have received the opportunity to further their studies. He laid the groundwork for an entire movement that relied on rational thought, discovery, and scientific innovation. He also proved that when religious and cultural knowledge is not only tolerated but celebrated, the results are beneficial to all society.

# AL-ZAHRAWI

## SURGEON EXTRAORDINAIRE

*The Abbasid caliphate wasn't the only important center of learning in the ancient world. Córdoba was part of the famous al-Andalus region in modern-day Spain. Al-Andalus was controlled by Muslims and was a seat of power, prestige, and knowledge for centuries. Muslim rulers of Córdoba quickly built it into a world-class city, where experts like al-Zahrawi lived and worked.*

### Court Doctor

Abu al-Qasim al-Zahrawi is known in the Western world as Albucasis. He was born in the year 936 in the town of Madinat al-Zahra ( "the shining city" or "city of the flower") near Córdoba. Madinat al-Zahra was a new city constructed to house the administrative offices of the kingdom. Al-Zahrawi grew up there, learning religion and the sciences. He was particularly interested in medicine and the art of surgery. In 961, at the age of twenty-five, he became the court physician for al-Hakam II, the caliph of al-Andalus. He also had many students, whom he taught medicine and who observed his techniques.

Al-Zahrawi made notes as he practiced medicine and wrote detailed instructions about every aspect of his work. He took case histories of his

patients and used rational inquiry to diagnose diseases and conditions. These direct observations became an impressive practical guide to medicine called the *Kitab al-Tasrif* (*The Method of Medicine*) collected over his fifty-year medical career. More than a book, the *Kitab al-Tasrif* is an encyclopedia of medicine, divided into thirty volumes that range from surgery to dentistry, nutrition to childbirth. It was finally completed around the year 1000.

## An Encyclopedia for the Ages

There is no doubt that al-Zahrawi was an accomplished doctor, and he understood both the human and animal body like nobody else during his time. A significant part of how we practice medicine today comes directly or indirectly from the *Kitab al-Tasrif*. It describes more than 300 diseases, their symptoms, and treatments.

The *Kitab al-Tasrif* also describes all of al-Zahrawi's invented procedures. He was an expert at the care of bones. He described how to repair a dislocated shoulder, using a technique Western doctors wouldn't learn until the late nineteenth century. He invented a procedure to remove shattered knee bones, something that wouldn't be introduced to the West until 1937. He was very interested in dentistry, and taught his students how to correct crooked teeth, put in implants, and make artificial dentures. He described several methods of plastic surgery, some of which are still used by plastic surgeons today. He also described medicines and drugs and wrote recipes for how to mix them in the correct manner.

## The Surgery Volume

The most significant volume of the *Kitab al-Tasrif* is the one dedicated to surgery and surgical instruments. Al-Zahrawi was the first surgeon to successfully operate on certain types of cases. He developed many new surgical techniques, such as the use of silk and catgut to stitch wounds. He developed special tools for drilling into skulls for the treatment of head injuries. Finally, and most importantly, he introduced more than two hundred surgical instruments, including tooth extractors, forceps, syringes, surgical knives, and saws. The *Kitab al-Tasrif* contains illustrations of these devices, many of which are still used in hospitals today.

### The Albucasis Legacy

Al-Zahrawi died in 1013, when the golden age of al-Andalus was almost over, and the kingdom was in decline. His hometown of Medinat al-Zahra was destroyed in 1010 during a civil war, and details about his life were lost. Nevertheless, his legacy is one of the most enduring in the Muslim empire. The *Kitab al-Tasrif* was translated into Latin in the twelfth century and became popular in Europe. It remained the standard medical text in universities for the next five hundred years.

# IBN AL-HAYTHAM

## REVEALING THE SECRETS OF THE EYE

*The scientific method is a staple of every school science lab, and the basis of how every scientist in the world conducts research. This method was first made popular by Ibn al-Haytham, a Muslim scientist in Egypt.*

### A Passion for Science

Ibn al-Haytham was born around the year 965 in Basra in what is now Iraq. He received a quality education and showed great potential as a scientist and mathematician. When he was a young man, he worked as a civil servant, but soon became frustrated because his real passion lay in science and discovery. He spent a large portion of his time working on his theories and discussing them with others.

### The Mad Caliph

Early in his career, al-Haytham was interested in not only science but also mathematics. Using his calculations, he thought of a way to control the Nile River in Egypt by building a dam across it and diverting the water. This seemed like an unbelievable engineering project to those around him. In 1010, al-Hakim, the caliph of Egypt—a patron of science and scholarship—heard about this plan and invited him to travel there to put it into action.

Al-Haytham was unhappy with his work in Basra, so he agreed. However, when he reached the river and reviewed it, he realized that his plan wouldn't work. And on top of that, he had another big problem: the caliph.

Caliph al-Hakim was known as temperamental and difficult to please. He had gained a reputation as the mad caliph due to some of his less popular public policies. Al-Haytham was worried about how al-Hakim would react when told the dam could not be constructed as promised. To avoid severe punishment he pretended to be mentally ill. Rather than punish him, al-Hakim had him locked up all alone for ten years.

### Arrest Leads to a Discovery

While imprisoned, al-Haytham observed a curious thing. He could see the inverted images of objects outside from a small hole in his wall. This interested him because of its marked difference with the popular scientific thinking of that time. The Greeks assumed that our eyes sent out rays of light with which we saw things. Spending years reflecting on this, al-Haytham realized that the inverted images from his wall meant that light rays came from objects outside and not from our eyes. He conducted experiments using a *camera obscura* (dark chamber), and wrote volumes on this topic. He conjectured that luminous bodies gave off light rays that could enter our eyes or bounce off other nonluminous bodies. This explained, for example, why the moon was still able to give off a weak light. His ideas were revolutionary: nobody had ever thought this before him.

### A Life Dedicated to Research

When the caliph finally died in 1021, al-Haytham was released. He made it his mission to continue researching and writing about optics and other important topics. He lived the rest of his days in Egypt, completing his written works, and tutoring others in a variety of subjects, until his death

in 1040. Over his lifetime, he wrote more than two hundred works. Of the ones that survived, some were on mathematics, others on astronomy, optics, and the human eye. He discussed concepts like refraction, depth perception, and even the speed of light. He used his mathematical genius to solve equations explaining the path of light rays, planets, and much more. He discussed optical illusions and why they happen.

Ibn al-Haytham's crowning achievement was a seven-volume set of books called the *Kitab al-Manazir* (*Book of Optics*), which he used to disprove all previous theories about the human eye and how it functions. Unlike other books, this was a real textbook with detailed descriptions of how to conduct each experiment, what apparatus to use, and how to analyze results. This insistence on continuous experimentation and the use of control tests is now well known as the scientific method.

### A Blinding Legacy

The *Kitab al-Manazir* did not become extremely popular until centuries after Ibn al-Haytham's death, perhaps due to the plague that swept across North Africa. The book was translated into Latin in the twelfth century, resulting in al-Haytham's ideas being discussed and shared widely all across the Western world. Many of the leading scientists were able to adopt these ideas about optics into their own work. The scientific method first utilized by al-Haytham became a widely accepted aspect of scientific discovery and experimentation. He is sometimes called the first true scientist.

In the fourteenth century, the *Kitab al-Manazir* was translated into Italian. This allowed the common man as well as several Renaissance artists to learn about perspective and depth, and utilize them in their art.

# IBN SINA

## THE PHILOSOPHER-DOCTOR

*A man whose statues grace the world today, Ibn Sina is better known in the Western world as Avicenna. He was equal parts philosopher and physician, often seen as arrogant and difficult, but forever respected for his brilliance and knowledge.*

### A Persian Prodigy

Ibn Sina was born in 980 in Afshana, a town near Bukhara, in modern-day Uzbekistan (Central Asia). The region was ruled at that time by the Saminid Empire, originally from Persia.

Ibn Sina and his family spoke Persian. His father was a high-ranking official in the Saminid administration, possibly a governor or tax collector. Ibn Sina was a highly intelligent student. While young, he moved with his family to the court in Bukhara. There, he studied religion, as well as Greek medical and philosophical sciences. He often used to stay up all night, thinking of philosophical problems and wondering about their answers. It is said that he became so well versed in logic that he was able to teach his instructors by the age of fourteen!

## A Miraculous Healing

At sixteen, Ibn Sina turned his attention to medicine. In two years, he had become a qualified doctor. One day, the ruler of Bukhara—the sultan—became seriously ill with a condition that his court physicians couldn't cure. Ibn Sina was called to the sultan's bedside and cured him using his superior medical knowledge.

The sultan was so grateful, he gave Ibn Sina a reward: the full use of the royal libraries. This allowed the young man to continue his quest for knowledge and learn more about the topics that interested him. He also became the court physician and slowly began to gain recognition there.

## A Change of Scenery

Unfortunately, Ibn Sina's expertise and fame resulted in his making enemies as well as friends. Some scholars and courtiers were jealous of his influence with the sultan. During this time, there was much political upheaval in the court at Bukhara. Ibn Sina's father died in 1002, and soon after the Saminid dynasty came to an end. Without the protection of the sultan, Ibn Sina was forced to leave. He traveled to various towns and villages, using his medical skills to earn a living. However, due to political intrigue, he was never able to stay in one place for too long. At several points in his life, he was jailed, once in a fortress. Often, he escaped in creative ways, including one incident where he disguised himself as a holy beggar.

He finally found a safe haven in Isfahan, in modern-day western Iran. There he spent the rest of his life, writing and healing the sick. He died in 1037.

## Famous Writings

In addition to his court duties, Ibn Sina loved to think deeply about life. He not only discussed his ideas with others, but also wrote them down. By the time he was twenty-one years old, he had begun his writing career.

Ibn Sina wrote several books about medicine. His main focus of interest was trauma, such as injuries and fractures, but he wrote about many other aspects as well. One of his popular books was the *Kitab al-Qanun fi al-tibb* (*Canon of Medicine*), which continues to amaze doctors and scientists today. Much of the medical knowledge we have now can be traced back to this encyclopedia, including identification of diseases and their cures.

But Ibn Sina was first and foremost a philosopher. During his lifetime, he wrote more than two hundred books about philosophy and religion. Some of the important topics he wrote about were humanity, society, politics, and ethics. He was very concerned about a human being's ability to learn and gain knowledge.

Ibn Sina wrote about these topics in the *Kitab al-Shifa*, which would become his most famous volume. Translated as *The Cure*, or *The Book of Healing*, the *Kitab al-Shifa* was an encyclopedia of philosophy modeled after the works of the famous Greek philosopher Aristotle. It consisted of four parts: logic, physics, mathematics, and metaphysics. This book became a long-term success. It was translated into Latin in the twelfth and thirteenth centuries and made an impact on the way philosophers thought about various issues during those times.

In this way, the philosophers of later centuries used Ibn Sina's writings to create their own ideas, just as Ibn Sina had used Aristotle before him. Today, he is well respected all over the world for his quest for knowledge and science.

# SALADIN

## RIGHTEOUS WARRIOR

*Saladin is widely known today in the Western world as a symbol of knighthood and chivalry. Plays and novels have been written about him, and movies have been made about his life. Yet few really know who this mysterious figure truly was, and what connection he had to the infamous Crusades of the Middle Ages.*

### From Soldier to Sultan

Saladin (Salah al-Din) was his title, which means "Righteousness of the Faith," but his name was Yusuf (Joseph) ibn Ayyub. He was born in a castle in Tikrit, near Baghdad, in 1137 or 1138 to a Kurdish family. His father, Ayyub, was in the service of the governor of modern-day Iraq, but the family soon moved to Syria. This is where Saladin grew up.

Saladin joined the military like his father and other male family members. He was a skilled horseman and learned how to fight. He accompanied his uncle Shirkuh on military expeditions under the banner of the emir Nur-al-Din. These expeditions

were to Egypt, which was being threatened by the Franks, the Christian rulers of Jerusalem. In 1169, Shirkuh conquered Egypt. That same year, Shirkuh died, and Saladin became commander of the forces in Egypt. However, like his uncle before him, he was considered a servant of Nur-al-Din. In 1174, Nur-al-Din also died, and Saladin seized his chance to be a ruler in his own right. He marched on Damascus. Soon, victorious over two major Muslim lands, Saladin became the sultan of Egypt.

## Unifying the Muslim World

As Sultan, Saladin had a formidable task in front of him. The world as he knew it was embroiled in a series of wars called the Crusades, in which Christian armies from Europe fought the Muslim rulers of Jerusalem for control of this holy land. In order to keep his power, and to defeat the rising armies of the Crusaders, he needed the various Muslim dynasties to unite. Through war as well as diplomacy, he succeeded in creating shaky alliances with most of the dynasties around him: Syria, Mesopotamia, Palestine, and Egypt. His reputation grew as a generous and kind ruler, ready to fight if needed, but not unnecessarily harsh or cruel. The Muslims in the past had been too weakened by their internal squabbles, but under Saladin, they were able to unite for a common purpose: defeating the Crusaders. Slowly, they all agreed to contribute their armies and wealth to fight a common enemy.

## The Crusades

Finally, Saladin could turn his attention to the invading Crusaders. Since his early days, he had been consumed with worry about non-Muslim, Western armies taking over Muslim lands. He fought many battles, laid siege to many cities, and succeeded in fending off the Crusaders on many occasions. The crowning achievement of Saladin was the retaking of Jerusalem in October

1187, a city that had remained under the rule of Western Europeans for eight-eight years.

### The Consequences

After Jerusalem's fall, Saladin was often depicted in the West as an evil, bloodthirsty man. News of his relentless pursuit of the Crusaders and the way he defeated them in battle quickly reached all corners of the Western world. Pope Gregory III called for a new Crusade, not only to take back Jerusalem but also to defeat the "monster" Saladin.

However, reality was very different. Saladin was not the monster they made him out to be. His subjects agreed that he was better than their previous rulers. Even as a conqueror, Saladin had no interest in unnecessary bloodshed. He'd previously spared the life of the European armies and their commander Guy de Lusignan. When he entered Jerusalem, it was expected that he would kill all those who'd resisted him. This was the practice of the times. But unlike Christian Crusaders who massacred Jerusalem's residents,

Saladin spared them when he conquered it. He wanted to be known for his generosity as well as his military strength.

All three major Christian empires—Germany, France, and England—responded wholeheartedly to Pope Gregory III's call. The third Crusade was led by England's king, Richard the Lionheart. Guy de Lusignan, whose life Saladin had spared earlier, also came back with an army. After many battles, giving victory and defeat to both sides, they finally agreed to a draw. Richard the Lionheart left the Middle East in 1192, and the Crusades officially came to an end. Contrary to popular stories, the two men never met in real life, but they were probably impressed with each other's military might and intelligence.

## An Abrupt Ending

Saladin was never able to enjoy his victories. The year after the Crusades ended, he died. Historians think it was due to the physical exhaustion of the battles that he fought almost his entire life. Saladin's legacy, however, endured. He began the Ayyubid dynasty in Egypt and Syria, which lasted more than sixty years. He became known, not only in the Muslim lands but also in the West, as a generous and chivalrous leader. His leadership and battle strategies are studied even today.

# RAZIA SULTAN

## THE FEMALE KING

*India was a powerhouse in the Middle Ages, with Delhi being its center. Over 320 years, five different dynasties made it their capital, from where they ruled much of the Indian subcontinent. The first of these dynasties was the Turkish Mamluks, and it had only one female ruler: Razia Sultan.*

### A Daughter is Born

Razia al-Din was born in 1205 in India, a first-generation Indian born of a Turkish father named Iltimush. Her maternal grandfather was the founder of the Mamluks and the first sultan. She was raised in the court—then located at Lahore instead of Delhi—and learned its inner workings from a very young age.

When Razia was six years old, Iltimush became sultan. He shifted the capital to Delhi and fought many wars during his reign to consolidate his power. He was a religious and intelligent man, and he filled his court with all sorts of people: doctors, scientists, mathematicians, historians, and scholars. Razia grew up in this rich and diverse environment.

### Sibling Rivalry

Razia spent her youth by her father's and brothers' sides. She learned

military skills just like the boys and watched her father rule in a just manner. Iltimush brought a lot of ideas from his Turkish background to the Indian subcontinent, including the greater freedom women had in that time period. He was also more in-tune with his people's needs. He installed a large bell on the palace gates, instructing anybody who sought justice to ring it so they could be admitted into the court. This and other practices Razia witnessed under her father's care showed her how to be a strong but kind ruler.

From the beginning, however, Razia knew she was never meant to be the sultan. Apart from the fact that she was a girl, she also had an older brother, Nasir-ud-din, who was the heir to their father's throne. Even though the Mamluk dynasty didn't function like a real kingdom with inherited positions, Iltimush always hoped that Nasir-ud-din would become his successor. The family's dreams were dashed in 1229 when Nasir-ud-din died unexpectedly.

### A Great Test

The next year, Iltimush had to leave Delhi because of a war in another area of the empire. He decided to test his daughter's capabilities by appointing her the governor in his absence. Razia rose to the challenge and proved herself to be a qualified and dedicated leader. When Iltimush came back a year later, he was impressed with Razia's performance. In 1236 when he was dying, he announced that he wished Razia to be his successor.

The nobles of the court were shocked and angered at the announcement of a female ruler. When Iltimush died, they refused to honor his wishes and installed Razia's half-brother to the throne. The new sultan was ineffective and weak. He saw Razia as a threat and planned to kill her. Razia used her father's ideas of justice to appeal to the people of Delhi. She walked on the streets and made impassioned speeches, reminding people of her father's wishes. She told them about the injustices carried about by her brother, including his plans to kill her. This was a bold strategy, but it worked. The people of Delhi began a revolt that finally removed her half-brother and made Razia the sultan.

### The Golden Rule

Razia became the fifth sultan of the Mamluk dynasty. She was unique in that era, not only because she was a female Islamic leader, but also because she came into power through the will of ordinary citizens. She made it her responsibility to always work for the people, rather than for the nobles. Her policies including the digging of wells and the building of schools, among other important public projects.

Razia was not content to stay within the walls of the court. She shocked everyone by giving up her veil and meeting publicly with men while doing the everyday business of the court. She was also in the forefront of all battles. She rode an elephant during wartime and led her armies like any other brave leader. Unfortunately, her actions did not make her a favorite of the elite class. She ruled for almost four years before the nobles rose up against her.

After several battles, she was killed, and another brother took the throne of Delhi. Razia Sultan, the Turkish princess and the Indian queen, thus became a part of the violent but important history of India.

# JALAL AL-DIN RUMI

## A POET FOR THE WEST

*The best-selling poet in the world is a thirteenth-century man named Rumi. His inspirational quotes are everywhere on the internet, and books about him have sold in the millions. Most of these quotes and books forget to mention one important fact: Rumi's faith.*

### Living in Shadows

Jalal al-Din Rumi was born in 1207. He came from a family of esteemed scholars who originally lived in Balkh, in present-day Afghanistan. His grandfather and father were both professional preachers with large followings. His father, Baha al-Din Walad, was known as the Sultan of the Scholars. Rumi therefore grew up in a very religious household as the son of a famous personality. His education was a mix of Islamic and secular subjects.

The Central Asian region where Rumi's family lived was a dangerous place during the thirteenth century. The ruthless Mongol armies were invading, and Baha realized that his community was no longer safe. Around 1218, he gathered up his family and followers, and traveled hundreds of miles to Nishapur in Iran. Rumi was around thirteen or fourteen at that time. The abandonment of his childhood home, and the violence he saw on his way, had a deep effect on him.

## A New Home

Rumi's father was never content to stay in one place. From Nishapur they moved to Baghdad, then Syria, and then many other cities. Everywhere, they were received with reverence and delight. The kings of each region showered Baha with riches to encourage him to stay, but Rumi's father was always worried about the Mongol army. Rumi grew older and got married, but still they kept moving. Finally, when Rumi was twenty-two, they traveled to northern Turkey, to a town called Konya. Two years later, Baha died, leaving Rumi to become the new spiritual heir.

Rumi no longer had his father's shadow to hide under. He needed to become his own man, worthy of the position he had been given. For almost a decade, he studied under religious scholars in Syria, then returned to Konya to lay down his roots. Slowly, he began to build a following of his own. He taught at religious institutions. He delivered strict and serious sermons that established him as a reputed scholar. His audience grew from ordinary people, to noblemen, and even to the king.

## A New Friend

In his late thirties, another dramatic change occurred in Rumi's life. A man called Shams mysteriously arrived in Konya, and the two became friends. This was no ordinary friendship, however. Shams was a wandering mystic, a religious scholar in his own right, but one who flouted religious conventions. Rumi began to spend long periods of time with Shams, learning and absorbing new knowledge. They formed a close bond of friendship that Rumi had been thirsting for. Tired of being a teacher, he finally found someone who was his intellectual and spiritual equal.

Unfortunately, Rumi's followers did not approve of this friendship. They saw their teacher neglecting his duties and were jealous of the closeness he shared with Shams. They saw him abandon his hatred for dance and music and lose some of his strict religious beliefs. They tried several times through protests and threats to get rid of Shams. Finally, the man disappeared about eighteen months after he had arrived, possibly kidnapped or murdered by Rumi's followers.

### The New Rumi

Due to Shams's influence, Rumi abandoned much of his strict, religious preaching. He was so agonized by the treatment his followers gave to his friend, that for years he was unable to do more than mourn. He went door to door as far as Damascus, in Syria, searching for Shams. After many years, he realized an important truth. What he had really been searching for was the divine, a connection to God and the universe around him.

Rumi became a poet, pouring his grief and longing into some of the most enduring Persian verses the world has ever seen. He often accompanied his poetry with song and whirling dances, so different from his strict preaching of previous years. His voluminous books—the *Divan-e Shams (The Collected Poetry of Shams)* and the *Masnavi (Spiritual Verses)*—contained explorations of age-old questions of self, identity, love, human relationships, salvation, and the nature of  God. He expressed a variety of emotions, from ecstasy to rage, from happiness to sorrow. He was inspired by the slightest thing, like the rustling of leaves, or the repetition of a goldsmith's hammer on metal. Leaving behind his conservative religious dogma, he focused on a mystical path full of music, dance, and poetry.

### Universal Appeal

Rumi died in 1273, soon after completing the *Masnavi*. Thousands attended his funeral and mourned his loss to Konya. Even after death, his impact continued to grow. His teachings became an essential part of Sufi Islam, and his group of followers became what is famously known today as the whirling dervishes, devotees who whirl, chant, and remember God. He is revered as an Islamic scholar and poet in his birthplace of Afghanistan as well as his adopted home of Turkey.

The popularity of Rumi's poetry resulted in its translation into many different languages, including Latin, German, and English. In recent decades, Rumi has gained recognition in the West as a poet with universal appeal. His verses about the meaning of life and love resonate with all people, regardless of their religion or culture.

# IBN BATTUTA

## WORLD TRAVELER

*The early fourteenth century was a time of discovery and learning through travel for many Muslims. Ibn Battuta joined this tradition early in his life and remained a world traveler until his last days. Some call him the Marco Polo of the Islamic world, but in reality, Marco Polo was the Ibn Battuta of Europe.*

### Pilgrimage

Abu Abdullah Muhammad Ibn Battuta was born into a respectable family in Tangiers, Morocco, in 1304. He must have been taught the typical subjects of mathematics, geography, religion, and more. He almost certainly received some training in Islamic law, since his father was a judge. Not much else is known about his childhood; his story begins in 1325 at the age of twenty-one, when he left his hometown to travel to Mecca for the hajj.

The hajj, or pilgrimage, is an important part of the Islamic faith. Muslims are enjoined to travel at least once in their lifetimes to Mecca in present-day Saudi Arabia, if they are physically and financially able to do so. In earlier times, many Muslims took this journey as a lifelong educational trip. They met scholars along the way and spent years in different locations, writing about their experiences. This is how they shared knowledge about the world with their fellow Muslims.

Ibn Battuta was no different. What started out as a pilgrimage to Mecca became a journey that lasted almost thirty years. During this time, he traveled approximately seventy-five thousand miles, from Spain in the west to China in the east. He walked, rode horses, and sailed on ships. By the fourteenth century, Islam had spread to a large portion of the known world—North Africa, the Middle East, and Central Asia as well as Spain—so much of Ibn Battuta's path was through Muslim lands. Along the way, he had many adventures, all of which he detailed in a travel journal of epic proportions.

### The Journeys

Ibn Battuta made several distinct journeys during his three decades of travel. First, in 1325, he went from Tangiers to Egypt and Syria, and finally reached Mecca. This trip took him sixteen months. Second, he went onward from Mecca and visited various cities, including Baghdad and Mosul, then came back to Mecca for additional pilgrimages. He stayed in Mecca for several years. Third, in 1328 or 1330, he took a sea voyage down the coast of Africa, returning by land to Mecca via central Arabia. But his most adventurous journey was yet to come. In 1332, he decided to travel to India taking a long-winding route from Egypt and Syria to Asia Minor, crossing the Black Sea on the way. He made a detour to Constantinople, then back again to the Indian subcontinent via Afghanistan. This trip took him three years to complete.

### A Second Home

India became a home for Ibn Battuta, when he accepted a job offer from Muhammad bin Tughlaq, the sultan of Delhi, as a local judge. This was a difficult job, for the sultan was a dangerous man with lots of enemies. In 1341, the sultan sent Ibn Battuta on a diplomatic mission to China, but a shipwreck destroyed those plans. For the next two years, Ibn Battuta traveled throughout India, and then finally went to China by himself in 1345. Then he traveled back to Mecca in 1346 via South India, Persia, Egypt, and Syria to perform another pilgrimage. In 1349, he reached home in Morocco, only to find that his parents had died from the plague. The next year, he briefly visited Granada, in present-day Spain, and then in 1353 he began his final trip: a caravan journey across the Sahara Desert to West African Mali. In 1355, he returned home to Morocco for good.

## One Journal

In 1356, Sultan Abu Inan, the ruler of Morocco, ordered Ibn Battuta to dictate his travel memoirs to Ibn Juzayy, a young scholar. This was a common practice among travelers of the time, and such a journal—whether written by oneself or dictated to another—was called a *rihla* (book of travels). It was a form of Arabic literature that flourished during the thirteen and fourteenth centuries in North Africa, but Ibn Battutta's *rihla* was different from others in significant ways. It took two years to complete, and hence was a comprehensive volume rich with details not found in other travel books. His *rihla* was not only a record of a great traveler, but also a depiction of the people, communities, and cultures—and even plants and animals—he encountered along the way. It became the source of political, economic, and cultural knowledge for people then and now.

## Ibn Battuta's Adventures

A man who travels for almost thirty years must have had many adventures along the way. Ibn Battuta's adventures ranged from shocking to laughable. Near Delhi he was attacked by bandits and rescued by a villager. Once, a shipwreck left him with nothing but his clothing, and another time his ship was attacked by twelve pirate ships. No wonder he hated sea travel! He tried different foods, such as locusts in North Africa and horse meat in Central Asia. He saw Indian rhinos and mistook them for Persian unicorns. At the same time, he observed how people lived, worshipped, and worked. He met a number of scholars and spent years learning from them.

With seventy-five thousand miles under his belt, Ibn Battuta thus became the most traveled person in the Middle Ages, more than Marco Polo and many others. He died in 1368 or 1369.

# ZHENG HE

## ADMIRAL OF FLEETS

*The Ming dynasty was the last and perhaps most important dynasty of China. It ruled China for almost three centuries, from 1368 to 1644. From bloody wars to political power, one personality stands out head and shoulders above everyone else in the dynasty: Zheng He.*

### The Ming Army

Zheng He was born in the Yunnan province of China around 1371. His father was named Ma Hazhi, and from this name historians understand that the family was Muslim. Ma He had one brother and four sisters.

From childhood, Ma He led an adventurous life. In 1382, two important events happened that had a tremendous effect on him. The Ming armies invaded his home province of Yunnan because it refused to come under the rule of their emperor. In the same year, Ma He's father died, leaving his family poor and without means to support themselves. A year later, Ma He was taken by the army—or perhaps he ran away with it—and reached Peking. This was a large city, and more importantly, it was the court of Zhu Di, the prince of Yan, the fourth son of the Ming emperor. Ma He was sent to the court to be in the service of the royal household.

## Changing Leaders

For many year, Ma He lived in the court and worked hard. Because of dedication to his duties, as well as his ambition, he quickly rose in position at Lord Yan's court. He received military training and fought in battles with Lord Yan's troops. His excellent record made him a trusted adviser and commander in the army and Zhu Di gave him a new family name: Zheng. He was now to be called Zheng He as befitted his station.

At the same time, things were changing within the Ming Dynasty. In 1398, the old emperor—Lord Yan's father—died, and his grandson became the king. The new king was young, and his advisers tried to sway him into making unwise decisions. One of these decisions was challenging his uncle Lord Yan's rule in Beijing. A year later, Lord Yan decided to lead a rebellion against his nephew. Troops were sent to fight, and Zheng He was made one of the commanders of the rebellion. In 1402 Lord Yan won the war. He removed his nephew from the throne and became the next Ming emperor.

## China's Glory

The new emperor decided to show the world the power and glory of China, in a way it had never been shown before. He ordered the launch of ships that would sail the Indian Ocean, led by none other than his trusted commander, Zheng He. This choice wasn't based only on military capability. Many of the countries in the region were Muslim, and Zheng He's faith would make him an appropriate representative. The foreign rulers would trust him and listen to him.

Zheng He's first expedition consisted of sixty-two gigantic treasure ships, full of expensive items like silks and porcelains, with 27,800 crew members on board, consisting of not only soldiers but also all sorts of professionals such as doctors, interpreters, accountants, mechanics, carpenters, and astrologers. They spent two years at sea, and visited several countries such as present-day Vietnam, Thailand, Sri Lanka, and parts of the coast of India. The main goal of the expedition was to build new relationships with the region's rulers. With a new emperor, China needed to show that it was still a leading power. Countries that considered China worthy of respect began to send their representatives to Beijing again. They also began to trade goods with China once more.

### Incredible Experiences

The expedition was considered a great success. The emperor was very happy with Zheng He and sent him on six other expeditions from 1407 to 1433, the majority of Zheng He's remaining life. They consisted of visits to a number of places, including India and the Middle East, and part of the African coast. Zheng He did not only deliver the emperor's message to the countries he visited, but also gave political advice and military assistance. During one expedition, he captured a powerful pirate and rid the region of his notorious gang. During another, he helped stop a rebellion and put the rightful king on the throne. Every time he reached home from a sea voyage, he brought back unusual goods and exotic animals. Once, he brought home a giraffe, which amazed the Chinese so much they paraded it on the streets for citizens to look at.

Zheng He's secretary, Ma Huan, recorded every detail about the places they visited and the activities conducted there. This information provides fascinating information about life in Southeast Asia during the Ming dynasty. Zheng He died during the seventh and final expedition. Some sources say he was buried off the coast of India; others say his body was brought back to China to be buried. No further sea voyages were conducted by the emperors after his death. With him, ended the naval power and glory of China.

# ABDUL RAHMAN IBRAHIM

## PRINCE AMONG THE ENSLAVED

*Islam reached the Americas through an unfortunate source: slavery. Experts estimate that a large percentage of enslaved people who were brought to the colonies were Muslim. Only recently are some of the stories of enslaved people being compiled and shared. One such Muslim was Abdul Rahman Ibrahim.*

### Family Life in Africa

Abdul Rahman Ibrahimwas born in Timbo in present-day Guinea, in 1762. He was the son of a powerful ruler in West Africa named Ibrahim Sori, whose kingdom was called Futa Jallon, So his full name was Abdul Rahman ibn Ibrahim Sori.

Abdul Rahman had a large family, including several brothers. In his youth, he spent some time in Timbuktu, a flourishing cultural and trade center in Africa. There, he studied religion and became fluent in four different African languages, in addition to Arabic. When he was older, he returned home and joined his father's armies as a colonel. He also got married and had children. In January 1788, when he was twenty-six years old, his father sent him with two thousand men to protect the coast and strengthen their economic ties in the region.

### Kidnapped

The battles themselves were successful. However, when Abdul Rahman and his soldiers were on their way home, they were ambushed at a narrow mountain pass by the enemy. Abdul Rahman was captured, along with fifty other soldiers, and was made to walk a very long distance to the Gambia River, where a ship awaited. His journey on the water must have felt never-ending: the ship traveled one week on the Gambia River, then six weeks across the Atlantic Ocean to the Caribbean, and then another six weeks across the Caribbean to the Mississippi River. From there, he traveled by ship to New Orleans and finally to Natchez, Mississippi.

Abdul Rahman was now enslaved. Bound with rope or chains, hungry and weak, he was taken to his new home in Natchez, Mississippi, by the slaveholder Thomas Foster. When he insisted he was a prince of Futa Jallon, nobody believed him. Foster nicknamed him "Prince" and put him to work on the plantation. He ran away once but was unable to get far. He was returned to Foster and put back to work.

### Distinguished Service

Abdul Rahman proved to be invaluable to Foster. He was highly educated, thanks to his years in Timbuktu, and he was honest and hardworking. He soon rose to a position of authority at the plantation, and received many benefits from Foster, such as being able to grow vegetables of his own. In

1794 or 1795, he married an American-born enslaved woman, Isabella, and they had nine children together.

Foster allowed Abdul Rahman to go to the market to sell his vegetables. In 1807, Abdul Rahman met a white man named John Cox, who recognized him. Cox had been in Africa thirty years ago, lost and ill, and had been helped tremendously by Abdul Rahman's father, Ibrahim Sori. Cox immediately asked the governor of Mississippi to release Abdul Rahman from slavery, but Thomas Foster refused. Abdul Rahman was too profitable to him.

### A Local Celebrity

Cox continued to work for Abdul Rahman's freedom until he died in 1829. Then, his son continued the cause. Because of their efforts, Abdul Rahman became a local celebrity. A newspaper editor, Andrew Marschalk, was intrigued by Abdul Rahman's story and decided to help. He asked Abdul Rahman to write a letter in Arabic, which he sent to Morocco, the only African country with diplomatic ties to the United States at that time. Marschalk also wrote to Secretary of State Henry Clay, who agreed to send Abdul Rahman back to Africa in 1828.

Foster finally agreed to free Abdul Rahman, but not his family. Marschalk again helped, gathering donations and writing about the situation in his newspaper. The local communities quickly raised enough money to free Isabella, but not their children. The couple left Natchez. They traveled to Washington, DC, and various others states to raise funds to purchase their children from Foster. The newspapers published many articles about him. Abdul Rahman met important people, from abolitionists to politicians, including President John Quincy Adams. They all found his story fascinating and some even agreed to help him. However, they did not raise enough money to free the entire Rahman family.

In February 1829, Abdul Rahman, his wife embarked on a ship that would take him back to his home continent. He was in his late sixties, sick and weak from travel when he landed in Liberia. He died on July 6, 1829, without ever reaching Futa Jallon. Thus ended the difficult yet intriguing journey of this Muslim prince who was enslaved in the United States.

# NANA ASMA'U

## AFRICAN POET AND EDUCATOR

*Nana Asma'u grew up in Nigeria at the end of the eighteenth century. In her early childhood, she witnessed a bloody war that established her father as the ruler, also known as the caliph, of the areas comprising Nigeria and the Cameroon in western Africa. Her family, the Fodios, helped shape the spiritual and political landscape of the region for generations to come.*

### Family Circle

Nana Asma'u was born in 1793, the daughter of Usman dan Fodio, a well-respected scholar and leader of the Sokoto caliphate in what is now northern Nigeria. He believed in the equal education of women—something not very common during that time—and gave the female members of his family all the educational opportunities he could afford. As a result, Asma'u grew up not only learning her own lessons, but also absorbing the scholarship and wisdom around her. She was educated in religious studies and Greek and Latin literature, and became fluent in four languages (Arabic, Fula, Hausa, and Tamashek).

Asma'u was very smart and caring. She was a wife and homemaker but was also very much involved in the politics of her family. She worked alongside male members of her family during battles and gave political advice to her brother who succeeded their father as the caliph.

## Teaching through Verse

Poetry was an important form of self-expression in the region. Both Asma'u's father and her brother who succeeded him were writers of prose and poetry, in a tradition that went back generations. One of Asma'u's major contributions to her people was her poetry. She wrote almost a hundred poems, all dealing with the social and political conditions she saw around her. Some of her works are accounts of the many battles she witnessed as a child, such as the "*Wakar Gewaye*" ("The Journey"), which detailed the war she witnessed at the age of twelve. Others are sketches of the people around her, such as her father or brother. And others are religious in nature, where she teaches readers how to be good and avoid bad deeds.

## An Education Network

Asma'u wrote her poems for the average person. She wrote them not only in a literary language like Arabic, but more importantly in Hausa, the native language of her people. Her poems were meant to entertain, inform, and stir her readers into action. She wanted to do something with her work above and beyond creative self-expression.

The wars in western Africa were resulting in more and more women left alone to fend for themselves. She began the task of helping them through education, not only for themselves but for the entire community. Her family strongly believed that knowledge must not only be gained, but also taught to others. She would teach women important ideas through her poetry, and they would carry those ideas back into their villages. Slowly, she gained a following of women who viewed her as their teacher. Some would visit her from afar to learn from her, and then they would carry those teachings back.

This cycle created a network of education called the *yan taru*, which relied on *jaijis* (traveling female teachers).

In this simple yet effective way, Asma'u organized a system of education for women. It meant that girls who were unable to travel for any number of reasons wouldn't be deprived of an education. It also meant that ideas important to women were shared among them without interference from men. Nana Asma'u died in 1864, but the *yan taru* grew over time, and the traveling network was replicated by women in many other African nations and beyond. This organization and others like it still exist in Africa today.

# NAGUIB MAHFOUZ

## ARAB DREAMER

*The novel had a late start in Arabic literature, mostly because poetry has been the preferred genre of Arab Muslims for more than a thousand years. Naguib Mahfouz changed all that. He brought a new level of interest and craft to the Arab novel and began a literary revolution unlike any other.*

### A Wild Imagination

Naguib Mahfouz was born in Cairo, Egypt, on December 11, 1911. He had six siblings but grew up lonely because they were all much older than him. His family was of modest means and very religious. He received his early education at a local Islamic elementary school before going on to study at a secular high school. His mother would often take him to visit venues of Egyptian history, such as museums and pyramids.

As a child, Naguib loved to read. Detective novels were his favorite, but as he grew older, he also read English and French classics. They fired his curiosity and imagination and aroused in him the desire to become a writer. He was also deeply affected by the

Egyptian Revolution of 1919. He witnessed the violence and bloodshed firsthand and understood the ideals of democratic struggle. By seventeen, Naguib was a writer, even though he realized that it could never be a full-time career for him. He graduated with a degree in philosophy from the Egyptian University (now known as Cairo University) in 1934, then joined government service like his father before him.

## A Young Writer

Naguib started out by writing short stories. Soon, he progressed to full-length novels. He typically wrote at night after a long day's work. His initial novels were set in ancient Egypt during the time of the pharaohs, the first being *The Curse of Ra* in 1939. Later, he turned his attention to more recent times. He wrote novels such as *Midaq Alley*, depicting the vibrant yet dangerous alleys of his childhood neighborhoods.

During his government service, Naguib worked in a number of important positions, including university secretary, director of the Ministry of Culture, and head of the State Cinema Organization. His work enabled him to put his fingers on Cairo's pulse and keep up with the changes taking place in society. He considered cultures to be the shapers of destinies. He wrote a weekly column in a leading Egyptian newspaper, *Al-Ahram*, in which he shared his sociopolitical views. His reputation was slowly growing, but he was still not well known.

## Nobel-Worthy Stories

All that changed in 1957, when he published the first book in *The Cairo Trilogy*. This series was an epic story about three generations of a middle-class Egyptian family in the period between the two World Wars. In it, Naguib depicted the comings and goings of ordinary people, and how they reacted to change and modernization. He shed light on the unexpected influences of Western culture on traditional values. This trilogy was an instant success, bringing Naguib recognition from all parts of the Arab world and beyond. It was translated into other languages, including English, and was adapted into films.

In 1957, Naguib gained attention of a different kind. His novel *Children of Our Alley* was criticized by fundamentalists as blasphemous and was banned in Egypt. But by now, his fame was reaching beyond the borders of his homeland. He continued to produce books and short stories, some of which were published in serialized form in *Al-Ahram*. In 1988, he was awarded the Nobel Prize in Literature for his outstanding and vast body of works. He thus became the first Arab to receive this award.

### The Gift of Literature

Mahfouz died on August 30, 2006, at the age of 94. He left behind a rich treasure of Arabic writings, including thirty-four novels, hundreds of short stories, movie scripts, and plays. From humble beginnings and a local readership, he had leaped to international acclaim. When the Swedish Academy awarded him the Nobel Prize in Literature in 1988, they commended him for creating "an Arabian narrative art that applies to all mankind." The beauty of his writings came from everyday political and social commentaries, wrapped in the realities of Cairo life. Literary critics agree that Naguib Mahfouz was instrumental in bringing Arab fiction to the attention of the international literary community.

# NOOR INAYAT KHAN

## SPY PRINCESS

*Bravery and heroism cannot be taught. They come from the heart, at a moment in time when one thinks all is lost. Noor Inayat Khan was not a soldier or a warrior, but she found courage at a time when the world needed it.*

### A Quiet Childhood

Noor Inayat Khan was born on January 1, 1914 in Moscow, Russia before the start of World War I. Her mother was an American, white-skinned with blonde hair. Her father was an Indian Muslim, a Sufi preacher, and a descendant of the great Muslim ruler Tipu Sultan. He sang and played musical instruments with religious messages. Often, he traveled to other cities and countries to establish Sufi centers and perform in big concert halls.

Noor's family moved to London soon after the outbreak of World War I, and then relocated to France in 1920. She grew up in the outskirts of Paris with her parents and siblings in a house called Fazal Manzil (the House of Blessing). Her education consisted of a variety of subjects, including the Sufi Islam her father practiced. She was not an adventurous child. Instead, she was drawn toward music, art, and storytelling. She wanted to be a writer of children's stories. Her father's work attracted many people to their home in Paris, and she lived a happy yet secluded childhood.

## World War II

As a young woman, Noor spent years in music school perfecting her skills. She also studied child psychology at the Sorbonne in Paris. Her manner was always shy and reflective, and she preferred to spend time writing and illustrating children's stories for various magazines. Many of these stories received praise, and one was read over the radio. In 1939, World War II broke out, and Noor's life turned upside down. She had just graduated from the university. Unrest and danger were all around her in Paris. She decided she wanted to do something—anything—to counter the threat that Hitler posed.

Noor and her brother Vilayat decided to join the war effort. As they vacated Fazal Manzil and left with their family to go to a safer place in France, Noor witnessed bombing and fear. This only strengthened her resolve to help defeat Hitler's army. She escaped to England after the fall of France and joined the Women's Auxiliary Airforce (WAAF) in November 1940 as Nora Inayat Khan. She was one of the first women to be trained as a radio operator. She worked hard and earned good reviews from her supervisors. Her training with musical instruments made her fingers especially well suited to tapping Morse code.

For Noor, this was a challenging but important part of her life. At Fazal Manzil, she had been known as Inayat Khan's daughter, someone removed from the average person. After graduation, she had tried to become a writer, but the war had cut short her ambitions. Now at WAAF, she tried to leave her real identity behind and become known for her skills as a radio operator. She communicated with pilots and helped send important information to them.

## A New Job

In 1942, Noor was accepted into a new sort of war effort: intelligence, also

known as spying. She quickly progressed in her assignments, until she
was part of a select group of women
who learned secret code. Many of
her supervisors thought she was
unsuited for spying, especially since
she seemed shy and scared. Still,
there was an urgent need for workers
despite their shortcomings. Noor was

a skilled radio operator and fluent in French. She was selected for the most
dangerous mission of all: infiltrating Nazi-occupied France and transmitting
their plans back to the Allies (the countries fighting Hitler) in London. She
was the first woman to be sent on this dangerous task. If the Nazis found
her, they would have no mercy.

Noor worked in Paris, the city she'd known most of her life. Her code
name was Madeleine. Her shy and quiet personality was very different from
that of the other spies, but it helped her maintain her cover. Still, she was in
a very dangerous environment. The Nazis were aware that radio operators
were working in secret, so they often sent agents to capture anyone who
seemed suspicious. Only ten days after Noor arrived in Paris, the Nazis
discovered her group. Hundreds of people were arrested. Noor's superiors
in England urged her to return, but she refused. She knew she was the only
radio operator left in Paris, and her work was even more essential.

### Critical for the Allies

For months, Noor worked tirelessly to send radio messages to the Allies
informing them about Nazi plans. Between July and October 1943, she
transmitted critical information that helped the war effort in many different ways, such as revealing Nazi weapon locations, and helping thirty Allied

soldiers to escape. The Nazi intelligence agency known as the Gestapo were aware of what she was doing, but they couldn't locate her. She was quiet and quick and did her job extremely well.

Finally, in October 1943, the Gestapo caught Noor. They interrogated and tortured her, but she never revealed any information to them. She tried to escape twice, once by organizing other agents and climbing on rooftops. When she was recaptured, they transferred her to a German prison near the Black Forest and kept in solitary confinement for ten months. Later, the Gestapo sent her to the infamous Dachau concentration camp and executed her on September 13, 1944. Her last reported word was *liberté*, which means "freedom" in French.

### A French Heroine

Noor was awarded the prestigious Croix de Guerre, France's highest civilian honor in 1946. Three years later, she was also given the George Cross by the British government. She was one of only three women to receive this medal for bravery during World War II. In 2012, a bronze bust of Noor was revealed at Gordon Square in London, near where she lived as a child. This was the first war memorial dedicated to a South Asian Muslim woman. While short, Noor's life was full of courage and passion for the ideals her father had taught her: freedom, tolerance, and love for humanity.

# MALCOLM X

## CIVIL RIGHTS LEADER

*The American Civil Rights Movement may have been a local one, but it impacted the way human rights were viewed around the world. Malcolm X was an integral part of that movement.*

### The Littles

Malcolm Little was born into a Christian family in Omaha, Nebraska, on May 19, 1925, a time in US history when discrimination and racism were commonplace.

Malcolm's father was Reverend Earl Little, a prominent and outspoken community organizer associated with Black nationalist leader Marcus Garvey.. As a result, their family often received death threats, and they moved to different cities to try to be safe. Once, their house was burned to the ground. When Malcolm was six years old, his father was killed. His mother grew sick and was unable to support them. Malcolm and his siblings were put into foster homes.

### A Rough Youth

As a child, Malcolm was a good student. However, his teachers gave him no support or encouragement. One even told him he'd never become a lawyer as he'd hoped. Malcolm dropped out of school and went to live in Boston with his half-sister Ella at the age of sixteen. He turned to a life of petty crime and was arrested many times. He became the ringleader of a group of thieves and earned the nickname Detroit Red. In 1946, he was sentenced to ten years in prison. While there, he decided to turn his life around. He started reading and studying.

His brother Reginald told him about a new religious movement called Nation of Islam. This was not the mainstream Islam that other Muslims practiced, but it had many similar ideas and teachings. Malcolm was very interested in this new faith. He converted while in prison, and spent years studying the religion. He also told other prisoners about it and encouraged them to convert as well.

### Nation of Islam

Started in Detroit in 1930, the Nation of Islam (NOI) was an important movement with the goal of improving the social, political, and religious lives of African Americans. During the cicil rights era, NOI was essential for the well-being of many African Americans. It built mosques and small Black-run businesses around the country.

The NOI promoted many beliefs that were similar to traditional Islam. Members believed in Allah, could not eat pork or drink alcohol, and maintained family ties. They rejected their last names as being from their past as enslaved people and replaced them with X to signify their lost African names. Malcolm Little thus became Malcolm X.

### A Community Leader

Malcolm X embraced his NOI identity with enthusiasm. He quickly rose up the ranks of the organization to become a minister and national spokesperson. His fiery speeches and continuous efforts resulted in a tremendous increase in NOI membership and worship centers.

Malcolm X was a civil rights activist like the country hadn't seen before. He was a charismatic leader and an incredible public speaker. During the 1950s and 1960s, during the heart of the civil rights movement, he expressed unhappiness about the treatment of African Americans in society. He made speeches and wrote articles about the urgent need for change. He also criticized other movements, most notably the peaceful movement started by Martin Luther King Jr.

Malcolm X felt that MLK's movement was not sufficient to make a change in American society. He believed that Black Power, Black identity, and Black nationalism were equally important goals. His beliefs, and the popularity Malcolm gained in the media, made him an enemy of the US government.

### *The Split*

By the mid-1960s, Malcolm X was breaking away from the NOI. He was still a staunch Muslim, however. He went on a pilgrimage to Mecca in 1964 and underwent another transformation. He converted to Sunni Islam, which is a more mainstream version of the religion than NOI had been. He also adopted a Muslim name, el-Hajj Malik el-Shabazz. He now directed his powerful charisma and public speaking skills toward a new ideology: racial unity and human rights for all. He became much more aligned with the mainstream civil rights movement led by Martin Luther King Jr.

Even though Malcolm X had now broken away from the NOI, he still had powerful enemies from all quarters, including the US government. He often received death threats just like his father had when he was young. On

February 21, 1965, he was assassinated while lecturing in Harlem. A few members of NOI were convicted, but to this day, questions surround his killing.

### A Controversial Legacy

Malcolm X's death did not stop his ideas from continuing, however. He had been dictating his life story to author Alex Haley in his final year. *The Autobiography of Malcolm X* was published just a few months after his death, giving people an insight into his thoughts and beliefs. Readers are able to learn from him and be inspired to fight for their rights no matter what the cost.

Malcolm X remains a controversial figure in the civil rights movement, but his passion for equal rights for African Americans was fueled by both his faith and his intellect.

# MOHAMMAD ABDUS SALAM

## FORGOTTEN GENIUS

*As a devout Muslim, Dr. Abdus Salam saw no discord between science and religion. In fact, he predicted the existence of the "God particle"—better known as the Higgs-Boson. Unfortunately, his genius was never appreciated.*

### Studies Above All Else

Abdus Salam was born in Jhang, a rural community in Punjab, now in Pakistan, on January 29, 1926. He belonged to a deeply religious Muslim family. His father worked in the education department of the Punjab government. He recognized his young son's zeal for learning and extraordinary aptitude for mathematics and science. He encouraged Abdus Salam to devote as much time as possible to his studies. Unlike the other boys of his age who spent much of their time playing in the narrow streets of his hometown, Abdus Salam worked hard and never missed a day of school. He was at the top of his class throughout his academic career.

At the age of fourteen, he sat for the entrance test for the prestigious Government College, Lahore, and scored the highest grade ever recorded in its history. When the news of his outstanding feat reached his hometown,

the streets were lined with cheering youngsters and elders alike, to welcome and honor him.

### In the Corridors of Learning

Abdus Salam was awarded a scholarship and enrolled in the Government College Lahore, University of the Punjab. After completing his master's in 1946, he was awarded a scholarship to Cambridge University, where he excelled beyond expectations and obtained a PhD in theoretical physics in 1951. While he was studying in England, the British left India and the new nation of Pakistan was created. He returned to Lahore in 1951 to teach mathematics at his alma mater. The following year, he was appointed head of the mathematics department.

However, his deep interest was research, especially in theoretical physics. In 1953, intense riots broke out in Lahore over the Ahmadiyya sect, a group of Muslims considered heretics (not following commonly held beliefs) by other Muslims. Abdus Salamwas a part of the Ahmadiyya community, so he decided to leave Pakistan to pursue a career in theoretical physics in London. He received a lectureship at Cambridge University in 1954, and in 1957, he was appointed Professor of Theoretical Physics at the Imperial College of Science and Technology.

### Contribution at Home and Abroad

Recognizing Abdus Salam's expertise in the field of science and technology, the Pakistan government appointed him Chief Advisor on Science Policy from 1961 to 1974. As a member of the Atomic Energy Commission of Pakistan, Abdus Salam played a crucial role in developing the nuclear energy and space programs in Pakistan. He became the founder and the first director of Pakistan's national space agency.

Because of his own experiences, Abdus Salam believed that scientists in developing countries urgently needed contact and communication with scientific peers in developed countries. He founded the International Centre for Theoretical Physics in 1964, in Trieste, Italy, and became its director. Abdus Salam worked tirelessly along with his colleagues, never going on vacation. Despite his workload, his students remember him as genial, supportive, and always available for discussion and problem-solving.

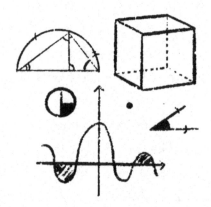

### Professional Triumph, Religious Betrayal

In 1974, Pakistan's government declared the Ahmadiyya community officially non-Muslim. They were barred from practicing their faith and proclaiming themselves Muslims. Brokenhearted, Abdus Salam left Pakistan. He was offered nationality by the British as well as the Italian governments, but, being a staunch patriot, he refused. He continued to call himself a Pakistani and did not break off his ties with the scientific community in Pakistan.

Abdus Salam's research in physics spread over three decades and ultimately led to the Nobel Prize. His pioneering work on unifying two of the forces governing the behavior of matter—the electromagnetic and the weak nuclear forces—is a landmark of twentieth-century science. In 1979, at the age of fifty-two, he was awarded the Nobel Prize in Physics, along with two other physicists. He thus became the first Nobel prizewinner from Pakistan, the country that rejected him, and the first Muslim to receive a Nobel science prize. At his award ceremony, he wore the sherwani, Pakistan's formal dress for men, and a turban. His banquet speech was in a mixture of Urdu and English, included quotes from the Quran, and explained that God was his motivation for seeking scientific truths.

Abdus Salam began suffering from a degenerative neurological disorder in the mid-1980s. As a result, he used a wheelchair. He retired from the Imperial College in 1994. He died on November 21, 1996, at the age of seventy, and was buried in Rabwah in his beloved Pakistan.

# FAZLUR RAHMAN KHAN

## STRUCTURAL GENIUS

*In mid-century America, as well as in other places, skyscrapers were seen as expensive, inefficient, and even dangerous. Then Fazlur Rahman Khan arrived on the scene. He took this conventional wisdom as a challenge and decided to change the architectural landscape of the world.*

### A Learning Mindset

Fazlur Rahman Khan was born on April 3, 1929, near Dhaka, in present-day Bangladesh. His father was a man of deep learning, who was a mathematics teacher and textbook author, and finally was assistant director of instruction for an entire district. Fazlur Rahman grew up in this atmosphere of learning and excellence. He was also very close to his father, who taught him to find the good in others.

As a child, Fazlur Rahman gravitated toward mathematics and science, but he also liked Bengali culture and poetry. Still, by the end of high school, he had to decide on a career. He chose civil engineering and entered Bengal Engineering College in 1946. Just a year later, the British left the subcontinent and his country was split into two during an event called the Partition. There was violence and fear among the people. Fazlur Rahman's hometown was now in East Pakistan.

## A New Engineer

After graduation from what is now known as the Bangladesh University of Engineering and Technology, Fazlur Rahman began designing roads and bridges for the East Pakistan government and taught at the university. But his dream was to study further, and he applied for various scholarships. Soon he received two prestigious scholarships to study in the United States, one of them being a Fulbright. In 1952, Fazlur Rahman left his home and traveled a long route through Asia and Europe before finally reaching the University of Illinois at Urbana-Champaign. Everywhere he saw the shared humanity his father had talked about.

Fazlur Rahman was an exceptional student. In three years, he obtained two master's degrees as well as a doctorate. His teachers had a lasting impact on him, especially those who taught structural design. After graduation, he joined Skidmore, Owings & Merrill (SOM), an architecture and engineering firm in Chicago. In 1957, when his visa expired, he returned to Pakistan, eager to apply the skills he'd learned in his birth country. He had goals of "building the world" and doing great engineering feats. After many disappointments, he got a job in Karachi, but it was nothing like he'd envisioned. His talents were not utilized, and the work was boring and repetitive. Disappointed, he decided to go back to SOM in Chicago.

## A Chicago Man

Fazlur Rahman was put to work immediately at SOM. He took on several challenges, such as how to design a skyscraper efficiently and safely. He decided that like the bamboo trees back home, the best design would be a hollow tube. They would better resist wind and seismic forces, big concerns for very tall buildings. Over time, he developed variations like the framed tube, and the bundled tube. He also worked on another addition: the trussed tube, using X-shaped steel beams on a building front to extend its strength.

Fazlur Rahman became the father of the modern skyscraper. After practicing on smaller and shorter buildings, SOM began taking on ambitious projects that shocked the public. The 100-story John Hancock Center in Chicago utilized Fazlur Rahman's diagonal tube system and became the tallest building in the world in 1965. The 110-story Sears Tower used his bundled-tube system and became a masterpiece of American architecture in 1974. The Sears Tower not only propelled Fazlur Rahman to fame but remained the tallest building in the world for the next twenty-two years.

## A Bengal Heart

Despite making the United States his home, Fazlur Rahman always kept his home of Bengal deep in his heart. In 1971, war broke out between the east and west branches of Pakistan. Heartbroken over the plight of his Bengali people, Fazlur Rahman founded the Bangladesh Emergency Welfare Appeal. He spent time and money organizing efforts to help refugees in Bengal. He also tried to convince US leadership to intervene to stop the war. When the war finally ended, and Bangladesh became a separate nation, he continued working to help its people any way he could.

All his life, Fazlur Rahman remained a proud Bengali. He would sing the poems of famous poet Rabindranath

Tagore and talk about his culture with family and friends. He always remembered the ideas his father had taught him and attributed his success to that early environment in which he was brought up.

### Skyscraper Legacy

During his career, Fazlur Rahman designed many buildings, from short to tall, from ordinary to incredible. In addition to the Hancock Center and Sears Tower in Chicago, he also designed the 714-feet tall One Shell Plaza in Houston, the Metrodome stadium in Minneapolis, the US Air Force Academy in Colorado Springs, the McMath-Pierce Solar Telescope in Sells, Arizona, and the Hajj Terminal in Saudi Arabia's busy airport in Jeddah.

Fazlur Rahman died before his time from a heart attack on March 27, 1982, at the age of fifty-two. But his legacy is powerful and enduring. His tube designs were game-changers, since they led to a rethinking of how tall buildings should be created. Every single skyscraper built from the time of the Sears Tower onward uses his designs in some form. Rather than being defunct as many predicted in the 1960s, skyscrapers were able to get taller and more artistic, thanks to Fazlur Rahman's. Today, the most innovative buildings may receive an award in his honor, such as the Fazlur Khan Lifetime Achievement Medal, and many others. A sculpture of Fazlur Rahman stands in the Sears (now Willis) Tower as a nod to this great man's achievements.

# AYUB KHAN OMMAYA

## THE BRAIN EXPERT

*The mysteries of the brain, and how it behaves when diseased, hurt, or injured, have been laid bare today thanks to modern technology. A major contributor to these understandings is a man from Pakistan named Ayub Khan Ommaya.*

### Smarter Than Anyone Else

Ayub Khan Ommaya was born in Mian Chanuu, in what is now Pakistan, on April 14, 1930. From his earliest days, Ayub was aware of different faiths and cultures. His father was a devout Sufi Muslim from the northwestern part of Pakistan, while his mother was a Catholic from France. The couple made sure Ayub and his siblings were exposed to different religious beliefs, so that they could understand various perspectives and world views.

Ayub was a brilliant student. As a youth, he read an article about experiments on epilepsy patients and became interested in the functions of the brain. He decided to pursue studies in neuroscience. He graduated from King Edward Medical College in Pakistan in 1953. There he not only excelled in studies but also sports, such as swimming and boxing, and other activities such as singing and playing the piano. After graduation, he received the prestigious Rhodes scholarship and headed to Oxford University in England. On his way, he stopped in Italy for several weeks to train as an opera singer.

## Becoming a Neurosurgeon

At Oxford, Ayub quickly got to the serious business of studying neuroscience. His teacher was the famous Dr. Joseph Pennybacker, a top neurosurgeon in Great Britain. Under the mentorship of Pennybacker, Ayub became an accomplished neurosurgeon. After completing his training, he went back to Pakistan, but couldn't find a job that equaled his qualifications. Disappointed, he decided to leave the country he loved so much and look for opportunities elsewhere.

Ayub arrived in the United States in 1961 as a visiting scientist at the National Institutes of Health. He began teaching at George Washington University in 1970 and advanced to chief of neurosurgery in 1974. Three years later, he took part in a surgery that catapulted him to fame. A thirty-four-year-old man suffered from a growing mass of blood vessels deep inside his brain that threatened to paralyze and kill him. This seemingly impossible case was brought before a team of George Washington University surgeons, led by Ommaya. He decided to stop the patient's heart, remove all the blood from his body, and return it once the surgery was complete.

This brave procedure had never been done before. The surgeons worked for nineteen hours under intense conditions, untangling the mass of snake-like blood vessels from the patient's brain, without stopping to eat or rest. Nobody was sure if the patient's brain could be revived after this process, but Ayub was successful. The surgery marked a new milestone not only for his career, but also for the field of neurosurgery.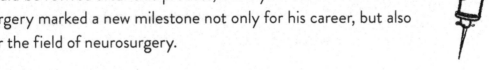

## The Ommaya Reservoir

In the 1960s, Ayub worked with many patients with brain diseases like cancer and tumors. He saw how difficult it was to deliver medicines directly into patients' brains. Infections would develop. In 1963, he invented a plastic dome-like device that can be inserted under the scalp to deliver chemotherapy and take samples of spinal fluid.

This device, called the Ommaya Reservoir, is a game-changer in cancer treatment. It has revolutionized the way brain tumors and cancers are treated, increasing safety and decreasing the risk of infection. It is a commonly used device in hospitals around the world, due to its benefits over other methods of delivering medicine.

### Research in Brain Injury

Dating from his Oxford days, Ayub was most interested in the topic of brain injuries, and how to prevent them. From 1980 to 1985, he was made chief medical adviser to the US National Highway Traffic Safety Administration. In this position, he commissioned a report on brain damage titled *Injury in America*. From the recommendations of this report came the National Center for Injury Prevention and Control, an agency Ayub was instrumental in getting initially funded and organized.

His research of brain injury had far-reaching consequences for the world. He developed the centripetal theory of traumatic brain injury, which allowed scientists to understand how brains are affected by blunt-force trauma. He conducted research to understand the effects of whiplash, leading to an improvement in safety devices in vehicles all over the world. He also worked on injuries of military personnel, helping scientists understand the long-term effects of war. He even invented an inflatable collar similar to an airbag for motorcycle helmets.

### A Sad Twist of Fate

Ayub found the intersections of brain, consciousness, science, and religion very interesting. He wrote hundreds of articles and taught many courses about these important subjects. As a Muslim, he believed strongly in the connections between science and Islam, and often urged the study of both as equally valid and essential to our understanding of life. At the same time, he was a friendly, outgoing person who would often surprise patients by singing an operatic aria loudly before a surgery.

After a productive career as one of the leading neurosurgeons and brain injury experts in the world, Ayub Khan Ommaya retired from George Washington University in 2001. Soon after, he developed symptoms of another devastating brain disease, Alzheimer's. For someone who had made the brain a central part of his life, this must have come as a big shock. He and his family decided to return to Pakistan so that he could live the remainder of his days in his birthplace. He died on July 11, 2008. in Islamabad, from complications of Alzheimer's.

# FAROUK EL-BAZ

## MISSION CONTROL

*From the Apollo missions to Star Trek, one name offers a deep, comforting presence to the field of both space and earth sciences: Farouk El-Baz.*

### Watching the Nile

Farouk El-Baz was born in Zagazig, a small village in Lower Egypt on January 2, 1938. His father was a teacher and a scholar of Islamic laws. El-Baz spent his early years of schooling in Damietta, a small port city near the Nile River. Every summer as a child, he'd watch the Nile flood, its waters brown with soil particles. There were also animals such as crocodiles, and plants from far away regions of Africa that were carried in the mighty river's water.

### A Thirst for Knowledge

Later, when his family moved to Cairo, El-Baz explored nearby mountains and caves. All these childhood experiences made him very interested in earth sciences. When he graduated from high school, he decided to study geology, chemistry, biology, and mathematics in depth. In 1958, he received a bachelor's degree in science from Ain Shams University in Cairo.

Not ready to complete his quest for knowledge, El-Baz left for the United States for higher education. In 1961, he received a master's degree in geology from the Missouri University of Science and Technology, and three years later a PhD. He conducted part of his research work at M.I.T. and interacted with the brightest minds in the country.

### Traveling Far and Wide

After completing his studies and teaching at Heidelberg, Germany, for more than a year, El-Baz decided to go back to Egypt. He loved his country and wanted to be able to contribute to its progress. His dream was to establish a school for economic geology there. However, this turned out to be a very difficult task. He got a job in Egypt as a teacher of chemistry, but nothing more. Frustrated and disappointed, he returned to the United States in 1967.

While looking for jobs, he saw a notice for a position at NASA. The Apollo space program was looking for geologists to study lunar surfaces and help find potential landing spots. Despite knowing nothing about the moon, he decided to apply. Due to his expertise in geology, he soon became secretary of the Lunar Site Selection Committee for all six moon landings.

### The King

From 1967 to 1972, El-Baz helped NASA identify landing sites for the Apollo missions. He trained astronauts in collecting data about the lunar surface by visual observation and with space photography while in orbit around the moon. He showed them which kind of rocks to gather from the moon surface and how to collect lunar soil. He was part of Mission Control when Neil Armstrong and Apollo 11 reached the moon for the first time. He was also there for every other moon landing.

El-Baz was affectionately nicknamed "the king" by his astronaut students, after King Farouk, who ruled Egypt during World War II. He was a very good teacher; while circling the moon, the pilot of the Apollo 15 said, "After the king's training, I feel like I've been here before."

### Learning about Deserts

After the Apollo missions ended, El-Baz moved on to other projects, including working at the Smithsonian Institution in Washington, DC. In 1974, he was called back to Egypt by then President Anwar Sadat to establish a desert research program. He would go with his team to the Egyptian deserts and study sand dunes to find information about how they were formed. He theorized that water was usually present under deserts, and he worked extensively to study desert formations. He used a process called "remote sensing" in which radar and satellite images are used to see under the surface of the earth.

Over the next few years, El-Baz explored major deserts in Egypt, India, China, Sudan, Oman, the United Arab Emirates (UAE), and Chad. Using remote sensing, he was able to locate ground water in Oman, UAE, and Egypt. He was appointed science adviser to President Anwar Sadat of Egypt from 1978 to 1981.

### Water Is Life

El-Baz firmly believes that access to water can solve many of the world's problems, such as war and poverty. He has made it his life's mission to convince governments and organizations to invest in drilling wells in desert areas. Because of his efforts, countless wells have been dug in various arid regions of the world. In 1986, he established the Center for Remote Sensing at

Boston University to study groundwater and other natural resources. Today, he serves as the center's director, and frequently travels to other countries to convince governments to drill more wells and locate water resources.

### Awards and Honors

El-Baz has received numerous awards from all across the world. The most noteworthy include NASA's Apollo Achievement Award and Egypt's Order of Merit. The Geological Society of America hosts the annual Farouk El Baz Award for Desert Research for scholars and experts. To honor him, the popular TV series *Star Trek: The Next Generation* introduced a shuttlecraft named El-Baz. An asteroid, discovered in 1978, was named 7371 El-Baz to honor this prolific and passionate earth scientist.

# FATIMA MERNISSI

## ISLAMIC FEMINIST

*Traditional Islamic societies can be very patriarchal, which means they tend to favor men over women. Fatima Mernissi was one of the earliest protestors of these social norms. She wanted to use the written word to change mindsets and cultures that went back millennia. Despite the odds, she proved it could be done.*

### Changing Times

Fatima Mernissi was born on September 27, 1940, in Fez, Morocco. She grew up in her parents' and grandparents' homes, within the harem quarters. Harems are traditional, secluded areas of an Arab home where women and children live, away from the presence of men. While harems are no longer common, they were an integral aspect of Arab households for centuries.

Fatima was an inquisitive child who did not like the confines and limitations of the harem. Fortunately for her, things were changing in the Arab world. Unlike her mother and grandmother, Fatima became part of the first generation of Arab women who were allowed out of the harem to study in an external school, receiving a degree in sociology from Mohammed V University. Later, she traveled to Paris to study political science at the Sorbonne. Then she set her sights on the United States. She earned her PhD from Brandeis University in Waltham, Massachusetts.

## Writing about the Harem

By 1974, Fatima was back in Morocco, teaching sociology and other subjects at her alma mater. Still, she was always thinking about her childhood in the harem. She wanted to explore the ways that women in some Muslim societies didn't have enough freedom because of social norms. She decided to do research about this important topic. In 1975, she wrote her first book, titled *Beyond the Veil*. This became a groundbreaking work in which Fatima explained that the oppression of Muslim women did not come from the religion of Islam, but rather from the attitudes of power-hungry men.

Nobody had written things like these before in the Arab world, and Fatima became an instant target of people who criticized her. Some thought she was maligning her own religion. Others thought she would bring shame to the Arab people. Rather, Fatima was doing something else. She was shedding light on the important difference between culture and faith. She insisted that Islam itself did not view women as inferior, but men did.

## Building a Field of Study

*Beyond the Veil* became a classic. It was revised and published in both England and the United States, leading to a higher profile for Fatima. But she was only getting started. She wrote several more books about the topics she was interested in. One of these, *Doing Daily Battle*, was based on interviews of Moroccan women who were asked about the struggles they faced in their lives. Another, *Scheherazade Goes West*, theorized that Western cultures also have harems for women, although they are more metaphorical than physical. All her major books have been translated into other languages, such as English, German, Dutch, and Japanese.

Fatima was mainly an academic who developed Islamic feminism as a subject to be studied and researched. Yet, her 1990 book, *The Forgotten Queens of Islam*, became extremely popular among average readers. Written after the election of Benazir Bhutto, Pakistan's first female prime minister, this book reviews the place of female leadership in early Islamic history. When some Muslims objected to Benazir's election as being invalid because of her  gender, Fatima showed by facts and historical research that Muslim women have been equal to men since the origin of Islam.

### This is Just the Beginning

Fatima Mernissi became a pioneer of Islamic feminism, a term that her mother's generation had never even heard of. She used her experiences to jump-start a sociological movement that would grow and expand over the decades. The goal of her writings was to shed light on the contributions of Muslim women, and to remind them of the power Islam awarded them. She also hoped to show the rest of the world that Muslim women were not as oppressed or incapable as the media and popular stories portrayed them. For her work, she was awarded many prizes, including Spain's Prince of Asturias Award for Literature in 2003.

Fatima died on November 30, 2015, at the age of seventy-five. She left behind a legacy that only continues to grow. She inspired countless other Muslim women to carry on the mantle of study and become scholars in their own right. Not all of them agree with her, but they see her as a starting point for their own discoveries and theories. Today, Islamic feminism isn't a strange or controversial thing, but rather a legitimate field of study due in large part to Fatima's contributions.

# MUHAMMAD YUNUS

## A BANKER TO THE POOR

*Muhammad Yunus grew up surrounded by poverty, but he used that to motivate himself. He asked deep questions such as, why are some people poor, and how can their conditions be improved? Rather than giving up in the face of such impossible queries, he decided to provide answers himself.*

### Lessons from the Roof

Muhammad Yunus was born in Bathua, a village in the outskirts of Chittagong, British India, on June 28, 1940. In 1944, the family moved to Chittagong, where his father opened a small jewelry business in a busy commercial area. He ran the business from the first floor of their two-story house. The family, consisting of nine siblings and parents, lived on the second floor. Their roof had a railing around it, and Yunus and his siblings would play there, often watching their father's customers and the busy scene on the street below. In 1947, the British left India and created a country with two parts: East and West Pakistan. The Yunus family lived in East Pakistan.

Yunus was a gifted student. He excelled at academics, and also participated wholeheartedly in extracurricular activities. He became an active Boy Scout and traveled widely to participate in Scout Jamborees as far away as Canada. As a child, he saw his mother, Sufia Khatun, always helping the poor. This impressed him deeply. He studied economics at Dhaka University, earning a bachelor's degree in 1960 and then a master's in 1961. Following graduation, he was appointed to teach economics at Chittagong College.

### Dream of a Poverty-Free World

In 1965, Yunus received a Fulbright scholarship to study economics at Vanderbilt University in the United States. While working toward a doctorate, he was an assistant professor of economics at Middle Tennessee State University. For him, getting used to Western culture on and off campus was an education in itself. He received his PhD in economics in 1969 and witnessed from afar the liberation of East Pakistan into a new country: Bangladesh. In 1972, he returned to Bangladesh as it struggled to establish itself. There, he joined the economics department at the University of Chittagong.

This job was another eye-opener for him. While traveling to and from his university, he observed the worst kind of poverty, especially in rural areas. Bangladesh is prone to seasonal floods and tidal waves. To make matters worse, a severe famine struck the country in 1974. The poor were barely alive. Many were dying of starvation.

Yunus realized that the economics taught in the classroom had no practical solution for the inherited poverty of the hapless villagers. On his fact-finding trips with his university colleagues and students, he discovered that the poor were always in debt. Most of these debtors were women. One woman his team interviewed made bamboo stools. To buy the bamboo, she was forced to borrow from money lenders at exorbitant rates. When she returned the money, she had almost nothing left as profit..

### *Taking a Leap of Faith*

This was the story of the villagers: they were enslaved to the money lenders and with no way out of poverty. Yunus believed that even a small amount of money could make a big difference to a poor person. In 1976, he decided to loan the equivalent of twenty-seven dollars of his personal funds to forty-two such women in the village of Jobra to help them out of the clutches of the loan sharks. He thought this would also enable them to reduce their poverty. The loan had to be returned whenever it was possible, and no interest would be charged. However, to get another loan, the previous one had to be paid off. With his connections and conviction, he was able to lay the foundation of microcredit and microfinancing. Everyone was skeptical about the repayments. Yunus himself was not sure it would work, but he wanted to try. The results were astounding: 98 percent of the borrowers repaid the loan, because this was their only chance of getting out of poverty.

Thus, the Grameen (of the Village) Bank was born. Each village selected for the microcredit program had its own branch of the bank. The beneficiaries of the scheme were women, the least visible and the most exploited in Bangladeshi society. Yunus empowered them so they were able to borrow small amounts that suited them. At the same time, they were able to learn a few financial principles and manage on their own. There came about notable changes in the lives of the villagers. They would not go hungry, and children could go to school. If any emergency came up, they could borrow money and repay later.

### The Laurels

Yunus established the Grameen Bank officially in 1983. He was able to find support for the bank from the World Bank, USAID, the Ford Foundation, and other sources. The bank is owned by the borrowers, most of whom are women. The bank also began investing into other ventures and industries, with the aim of improving the conditions of poor people. What had started with small personal loans was extended to long-term loans for self-employment, housing, health, education, and so much more.

Mohammad Yunnus received many international awards for his ideas, including the Sydney Peace Prize, the Seoul Peace Prize, and the Presidential Medal of Freedom from US President Barack Obama. His concept of microfinancing for poverty alleviation has been adopted (or adapted) in more than four hundred countries around the world. Several other banks now operate on the same principles. He was awarded the Nobel Peace Prize in 2006, along with Grameen Bank, for their effort "to create economic and social development from below."

# MUHAMMAD ALI

## THE CHAMPION

*Cassius Clay knew he was the greatest boxer the world had ever seen. But then religion and politics intervened. He changed his name, his faith, and even his political views. Finally, he understood what being the greatest really meant.*

### A Fun-Loving Kid

Cassius Marcellus Clay Jr. was born to Christian parents in Louisville, Kentucky, on January 17, 1942. He was a loud and rambunctious child, frequently getting into mischief and entertaining the rest of the household. He loved cowboys, and he was obsessed with Sugar Ray Robinson, the Black American boxer who came before him. He would listen to his fights on the radio and want to be just like him.

Cassius's father, Cassius Marcellus Sr., aka Papa Cash, was a painter. He not only painted signs on buildings and trucks, but also big murals on church walls, depicting religious figures from the Bible. His mother, Odessa Grady Clay, was a kind, religious woman who cleaned houses. The family lived in poverty, wearing secondhand clothes and eating simple meals. Cassius went to school, but he struggled because of an undiagnosed learning disability called dyslexia.

### A Stolen Bike

When Cassius was twelve years old, a chance encounter changed his life. His new bike—a Christmas present from his father—had been stolen, and he was looking for a police officer to file a report. He found one in Joe Martin, who, in addition to his regular duties, was also the owner of the Columbia Gym, the only nonsegregated gym in Louisville. Cassius vowed to Martin that he would beat up the thief, but Martin suggested he learn to fight first. The Columbia Gym was the perfect place to start, and Joe Martin the perfect teacher. Thus, Cassius entered the world of boxing, with Joe Martin as his first coach.

Although not a professional trainer, Martin had coached many kids before Cassius. He saw the young man's talent and promised to make him a star. In six weeks, Cassius was on *Tomorrow's Champions*, a weekly televised boxing program in Kentucky. He won that match, and Cassius's life changed. He finally had purpose and a way out of the discrimination of the American South. He could be like his hero Sugar Ray Robinson and achieve stardom.

### From Amateur to Professional

Cassius trained hard to make a name for himself in boxing. Soon, he was winning many amateur competitions against other young boxers. He went on to become successful at the Golden Gloves, a state championship for amateur boxers. He won six Kentucky Golden Gloves titles, and two national Golden Gloves titles, and finally went on to win the Light

Heavyweight gold medal in the 1960 Summer Olympics in Rome.

The Olympics launched Cassius into a professional boxing career. On the one hand, he still felt the racism of the segregated South—after winning the gold medal, he was still refused service in a "whites-only" restaurant in his hometown—but on the other, he saw the glinting fame of a boxing career. He decided to give it his all. He made his professional debut in October 1960, and immediately began winning titles.

### Signature Style

Cassius was usually considered the underdog in his early fights. In many of his wins, he would surprise a lot of people, including reporters. The way he fought in the boxing ring was also very unusual. He would loudly scold his opponents, calling them harsh words to make them lose confidence. He was also a poet, and he would make funny rhymes to sing before and during his fights in a loud voice.

One of his most formidable opponents was the ex-Mobster Sonny Liston, whom he beat despite all odds in Miami to become the heavyweight champion in 1964. This is where he coined his now-famous phrase "float like a butterfly, sting like a bee." The hands can't hit what the eyes can't see." Another was George Foreman, whom he beat in an exhilarating match, the "Rumble in the Jungle" in Kinshasha, Zaire, in 1974. Cassius was also known for his fancy footwork, so different from the heavy stomping of his opponents in the ring. He was unique, and he shook the boxing world.

### A Change of Heart

Like many African Americans in the civil rights era, Cassius was influenced by the Nation of Islam, a Black nationalist group against white supremacy. He was also disturbed by the history of his own name, which came from his enslaved ancestors' owner. In 1964, Cassius announced that he'd converted and changed his name to Muhammad Ali. People were surprised and unsure of how this would affect his boxing career, but Muhammad Ali didn't care. He continued to compete and win matches.

Another big decision would have more of a profound impact on his career. In 1955 the Vietnam War began, and all eligible American men were forced to serve in the military. In 1965 Muhammad Ali officially refused to be drafted into the US Army. Ali knew that this was against the law, but he explained that he wouldn't fight a war for a country that didn't give him equal rights yet expected him to lay down his life. This is called conscientious objection.

### Hardest Years

Muhammad Ali was now an outcast. His boxing championship and his boxing license were taken away. He was indicted, convicted, and sentenced to five years in prison. He was seen as unpatriotic by many Americans, and his popularity declined. Still, he continued speaking out against the war at college campuses and fought his conviction in the courts. Finally, in 1971 the US Supreme Court overturned the conviction, and Muhammad Ali was free to resume boxing without stigma. Some of his most exciting fights, such as the one against Foreman in Zaire, occurred during this second half of his career.

Muhammad Ali finally retired in 1981 at the age of thirty-nine. He had won the heavyweight championship title three times, with fifty-six wins and only five losses. *The Ring* magazine named him "Fighter of the Year" five times, more than any other boxer. Sadly, boxing had taken a toll on his health. In 1984, he announced that he was suffering from Parkinson's disease. He remained active on the world stage, lighting the Olympic torch at the opening ceremony in Atlanta, Georgia, in 1996. He became a philanthropist, spending his time and money for a number of important causes. In 2000, a federal law called the Muhammad Ali Boxing Reform Act was passed by the US government, protecting boxers' rights and giving them more oversight. It is popularly known as the Ali Act.

From his dedication as a sportsman, to his standing up for what was right despite the consequences, Muhammad Ali became an all-American role model for youth around the world. In 2005, he received the Presidential Medal of Freedom in 2005 from US President George W. Bush, and the President's Award from the NAACP in 2009. He died on June 3, 2016, at the age of seventy-four. His funeral was attended by thousands of people, including past presidents and senators.

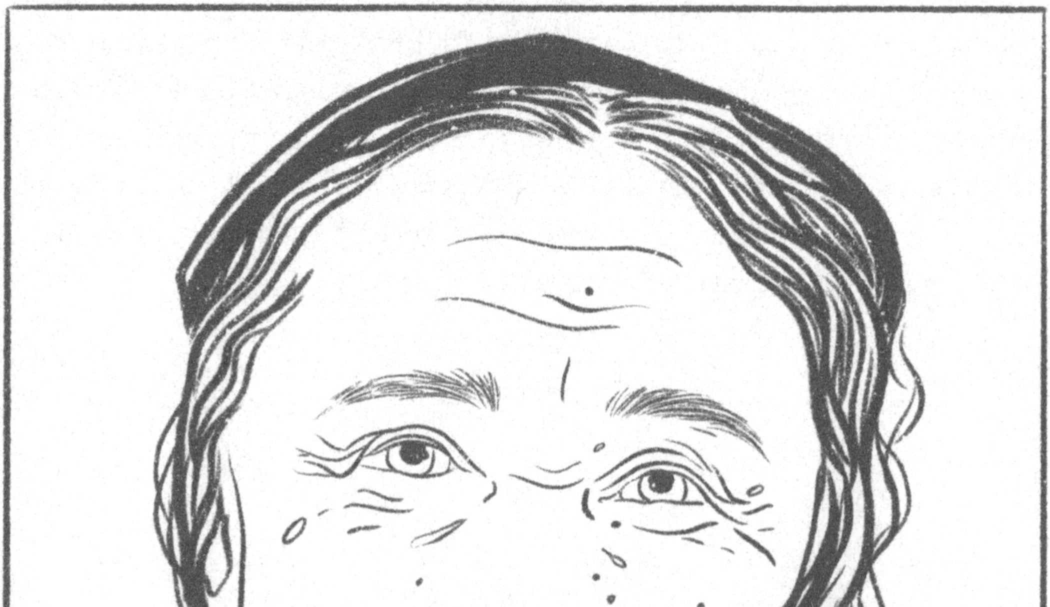

# REBIYA KADEER

## GRANDMOTHER OF STEEL

*Few in the Western world know about the terrible conditions under which the Uyghurs live in China. One woman made it her life's work to change that. Rebiya Kadeer knew she had little freedom and even less power to free an entire nation of people. That wasn't going to stop her.*

### Blessed Baby

Rebiya Kadeer was born on November 15, 1946, near the Altai mountains in the Xinjiang region of China. Her parents were descendants of migrants and refugees and traveled on these craggy mountains with a group of miners. On the day she was born, her father, an ex-soldier, struck gold unexpectedly. As the mining group's leader, he distributed the riches among everyone. After the celebrations, he predicted that his newborn daughter would always be a blessing for her people, the Uyghurs.

Rebiya grew up in an environment of political chaos. In 1949, China took over the Xinjiang region, routinely persecuting the Uyghurs, a Turkic-speaking Muslim population of Central Asia. By the time she was a few years old, her father had settled in a bigger city and started a number of small businesses. Rebiya saw violence and murder all around her, perpetrated by Chinese soldiers.

### A Tormented Life

Rebiya watched her parents, friends, and family struggle with increasingly difficult conditions under the Communist Chinese government. Twice, the family was banished from their home. They faced hunger, forced manual labor, and indoctrination. At fifteen she married, to help her family escape poverty. As she grew older, she began to protest the Chinese government's treatment to her family, her friends, and her neighbors. This often got her in trouble with local police, who would haul her to public market squares for physical punishment and humiliation. She had six children, all of whom would be forced to witness their mother's punishments.

The pain and humiliation only served to motivate Rebiya even more. She dreamed of freeing the Uyghurs from Chinese rule. But as a home-maker and mother, how could she undertake such an impossible mission? She began to secretly make clothing and shoes and sell them on the black market. With the money she earned, she helped those less fortunate than herself. Sometimes she used the money to bribe Chinese soldiers to release Uyghurs. Her activities made her husband furious. After thirteen years of marriage, he divorced her.

### A New Purpose

Rebiya decided to make a new life for herself, dedicated to the Uyghur people. She built a series of small businesses, including a laundry service. She traveled far and wide selling everything from sheepskin to carpets. It was unheard of for Uyghur women to conduct business, but she didn't care about social norms. In the beginning, capitalism was illegal, and the Chinese government had strict controls on buying and selling. Soon, however, the laws changed, and Rebiya was able to make business deals in plain sight. Before long, she was rich.

She married again in 1981. This time, her husband was her intellectual equal and a fierce fighter for the Uyghurs like her. He had previously been imprisoned and tortured by the government. Together, they vowed to do everything in their power to free their people. They protested in Beijing against the mistreatment and murders of innocent Uyghurs. They also continued working hard and making money, using the profits to secure the release of other jailed protesters.

## Success and Failure

Rebiya quickly gained popularity and recognition as an astute businesswoman, respected by both the Uyghurs and the Chinese. She entered the real estate business, constructing department stores and apartment buildings. She also started to trade goods with other countries in Central Asia. Before long, she was one of the richest people in China. She was also allowed positions in politics, where she continued to bring the plight of the Uyghurs to the public's attention.

But it was difficult to enjoy personal successes when her people were suffering. After the collapse of the Soviet Union, China cracked down on the Uyghurs even more than before, fearing that they, too, would seek their independence. Life became unbearable for the average Uyghur. In 1996, Rebiya convinced her husband to flee to the United States. In his absence, she continued protesting China's human rights abuses loudly and publicly. She also increased her philanthropy, organizing schools and business projects for the poorest citizens. In 1999, she was arrested and sentenced to eight years in prison.

## A New Chapter

In prison, Rebiya's health deteriorated. Her husband petitioned the US government to help. Finally, the Chinese relented and released her on medical grounds in 2005. Rebiya was exiled to the United States. She was happy to be reunited with her family, but she was determined to use this opportunity to promote the Uyghurs' cause from a safe, democratic country. She became the president of the World Uyghur Congress, an international group that fights for the right of that nation to be separate from China, and president of the Uyghur American Association. She traveled across the U.S. and America, and met foreign dignitaries, including President George W. Bush, continuing her fight for human rights and self-determination for the Uighur people.

The Chinese government labeled her a dangerous terrorist and demanded that she cease all activities. An assassination attempt was made in 2006, from which she escaped with injuries. Still, Rebiya's high profile work continued. She knew her own freedom meant nothing until her people were also free. For her tireless efforts, she was awarded several prizes by international organizations, and was nominated for the Nobel Peace Prize.

# KAREEM ABDUL-JABBAR

## FROM HOOPS TO BOOKS

*Sports is often the only path to college for poor kids. For Kareem Abdul-Jabbar, basketball was much more than a ticket to a better life. It was the path through which he could inspire countless other youth.*

### Growing Tall

Kareem Abdul-Jabbar was named Ferdinand Lewis Alcindor Jr. when he was born on April 16, 1947 in New York City. He was always a big child, and by the time he was a teenager, he was more than six and a half feet tall. In his early childhood, he gravitated toward sports like baseball, but was known to shoot baskets at a playground near home. In fourth grade, however, he honed his skills basketball while at a boarding school.

Over the next few years, Lewis trained hard to play this sport. By eighth grade, slam-dunking—an uncommon move at that time—became an easy feat for him at six feet eight inches tall. It won him a scholarship to a private Catholic high school, Power Memorial, in 1961.

### Early Wins

While at Power Memorial from 1962 to 1966, he led his school varsity team to a 78–1 record and two national championships. He made the all-city team

each year in high school and set a record for the most points scored by a high school player. Given his height, he received 4-F status, which enabled him to avoid the draft and being sent to Vietnam. By the time he was ready for college, the invitations were pouring in. He chose the University of California at Los Angeles (UCLA) because of its basketball coach: the legendary John Wooden.

Under Wooden's guidance, Lewis led UCLA's college basketball team, the Bruins, to three consecutive national championships between 1967 and 1969. During these years he won several awards and honors, such as the All-American, Most Outstanding Player, and College Player of the Year. *Sports Illustrated* named him "The New Superstar." He perfected his famous "skyhook" move that earned the envy of other players and the admiration of his fans. All this cemented him as a top player in the sport, one who'd be an asset to any pro-basketball team.

### Difficult Times

At the same time, Lewis faced many obstacles on and off the court. He was a witness to the often violent civil rights movement in America and the way his fellow Black Americans were treated every day. His rising fame pushed him to be a spokesperson for Black people, and he yearned to use his platform for civil rights advancements. But he didn't know how.

Although basketball provided a relief, it also had its low moments. His signature "dunk" was banned from college basketball in 1967. He got injured in the eye, resulting in games lost while he was absent. Most importantly, he witnessed a disconnect between the Christianity he was taught at church and the behavior of his Christian friends. All this had a deep impact on Lewis's spirituality. In 1968, after years of studying, he converted to Islam.

### Pro-Ball

After graduating from UCLA, Lewis joined the Milwaukee Bucks as a pro-basketball player. He immediately began leading the team to victory, winning several awards from the National Basketball Association (NBA).

When the Milwaukee Bucks became NBA Champions in 1971, he announced a name change. From now on, Lewis Alcindor Jr. would be Kareem Abdul-Jabbar, an Arabic name meaning "noble servant of the powerful God." In 1975, Kareem was traded to the Los Angeles Lakers, where he played more impressive games and made more records, aided by fellow superstar player Magic Johnson. By the end of his career, Kareem was the NBA's all-time leading scorer and held an unprecedented six Most Valuable Player (MVP) awards.

### Life after Basketball

Kareem retired from pro-basketball in 1989 at the age of forty-two. While he did some basketball coaching, he mostly went on to focus on other interests. He fell in love with reading and writing when he was a high school student and has written many books, including memoirs, essays, political articles, and a mystery series. He has also written for and acted in several films and television shows.

Kareem remains a beloved American sports celebrity. He uses his high-profile platform to bring attention to important social and political issues. He was appointed a cultural ambassador of the United States in 2012 and awarded the Presidential Medal of Freedom in 2016 by US President Barack Obama. He is also the founder of the Skyhook Foundation, an organization that provides educational opportunities to children from underserved communities.

# SHIRIN EBADI

## HUMAN RIGHTS DEFENDER

*Iran is a country with a history of women's rights abuses. From forced veiling to political violence, women fare worse than any other group under the country's recent authoritarian regime. Shirin Ebadi wants to change all that, and she's not afraid to fight.*

### Lawyerly Ambitions

Shirin Ebadi was born in Hamadan, Iran, on June 21, 1947, and was raised in its largest city, Tehran. She grew up observing the unfair, preferential treatment Iranian society offered to males. Yet her own father always treated her and her brother equally. Thus, in her childhood, Shirin developed a strong belief in the equality of genders, something that would become a hallmark of her adult work.

Following in her father's footsteps, Shirin studied to be a lawyer. After getting a law degree from the University of Tehran, she was hired at the Iranian justice department and held a variety of positions there. In 1970, at the age of twenty-three, she became one of the first female judges in Iran. So began her career in women's rights and empowerment. While she was at the justice department, Shirin decided to get a doctorate in private law in 1971. This degree and her experience in the government allowed her to rise to the position of Tehran city court president in 1975. Shirin thus became the first female judge in the country.

## A Revolution

Shirin married an electrical engineer in 1975, who supported and encouraged her work. Just as Shirin's career was getting started, Iran was going through turmoil and uncertainty. The Iranian people were unhappy with their monarchy and some wanted a government based on their religious principles. Finally, in 1978 Iran went through a revolution that turned the nation upside down. The shah (title given to rulers of Iran) fled the country in disgrace. In the beginning, Shirin was excited about these changes. Like her fellow Iranians, she wanted democracy in her country, rather than a corrupt monarch. She participated in victorious parades and shouted *"Allahu Akbar"* (God is greater) from the rooftops along with thousands of others.

Soon, however, Shirin realized that her dreams of a free and progressive Iran had been dashed to pieces. The new rulers who came into power wanted Iran to be modeled after a strict interpretation of Islam, which had no place for female leaders, especially judges. Shirin and other female judges were demoted to clerks in the same court where they used to be judges. Shirin resigned in protest and decided to become a private lawyer—another step she was denied. Her professional life halted, she spent time at home with her children, worried about her disappearing income. Slowly, friends and family started leaving Iran, for the safety and security of other countries. Shirin herself was adamant she'd never leave. She would stay and fight for the people of Iran.

### An Advocate for Civil Rights

Shirin's experiences after the Islamic Revolution made her understand the plight of other marginalized members of her community like never before. She wrote books and articles and became an expert on the everyday problems Iranians faced. A government decree prohibited her—and all female lawyers—from practicing on her own, so she joined an all-male firm in the 1980s and began working on human rights cases. After the death of the Ayotollah, restrictions eased, and Shirin was able to practice law on her own again in 1992. Many people came to her for legal services, and she defended them in court against the government. All of her cases were difficult, and a few became well known in the international media.

Shirin became known as the lawyer for political dissidents and prisoners. She worked on a team with twenty lawyers and fought more than six thousand political cases in Iran. Most importantly, her team did not charge any legal fees for these cases, since she knew how difficult it was for the families of victims to pay. She also fought against child abuse and child marriages.

### Imprisonment

Shirin came to be known in Iran as an enemy of the state. In 1999, she was found guilty of "disturbing public opinion" and jailed in the very prison where she often went to meet with clients. This was one of the most difficult times in her life. She spent twenty-five days in solitary confinement simply because she fought for justice. She became sick and suffered from hallucinations. Finally, help came from outside, and due to international pressure, the Iranian government released Shirin. Still, she was fined and her license to practice law was suspended for five years.

### The Highest Prize

The Iranian government may have tried to silence her, but the rest of the world was watching and listening. In 2003, while on a trip to Paris, Shirin learned that she had been awarded the Nobel Peace Prize for her civil rights work. She was shocked and humbled, especially when hundreds of thousands of people, mostly women, turned up at the Tehran airport to welcome her home and celebrate her victory. Shirin put the award money to good use. She created an organization called the Center for Defenders of Human Rights (CDHR) that became a major source of help for families of political prisoners and other groups, including the minority Baha'i community in Iran.

### Exile

Shirin Ebadi and her organization, CDHR, was vocally critical of the human rights abuses of the Iranian government. Finally, in 2008, the government shut down CDHR. She received threats to her life, and to the lives of her daughters and sister. Her husband was arrested, tortured, and forced to publicly renounce her. The following year, the government confiscated her Nobel Prize and seized her bank accounts, leading Shirin to flee to the United Kingdom. Since then, she has continued to live in exile. She spends her time working on human rights issues around the world and bringing attention to the Iranian government's activities. Her goal is to one day return to Iran, but for now, her work continues outside it.

# YUSUF/CAT STEVENS

## POP IDOL

*Music is sometimes considered forbidden by strict Muslims. Yet music has the power to motivate, inspire, and bring people together. Yusuf Islam found that power through his lyrics, and he wanted to use it for a better understanding of his faith.*

### Glitzy London

Yusuf Islam was born Stephen Demetre Georgiou in London, England, on July 21, 1948. His father was a Greek Cypriot, and his mother was Swedish. He was raised Greek Orthodox but attended a Catholic elementary school. His family ran a restaurant in the heart of the city's theater district. They lived in an apartment above it, and everyone was expected to pitch in. The glamourous world of music and glitz was a constant presence in the neighborhood. It fueled young Stephen's inclination and talent for music. He loved the newly famous Beatles and in 1963 convinced his father to buy him a guitar.

Stephen studied at the Hammersmith College of Art, wanting to become a cartoonist at one point. While still at college, he started writing songs and performing solo in coffee houses and bars. He soon landed a publishing deal as a songwriter. At the age of seventeen, he wrote a song titled

"The First Cut Is the Deepest," which rose to number eighteen on the UK charts for singer P. P. Arnold. In 1966, Stephen landed a record deal with Decca Records and released his own single, "I Love a Dog," which reached number twenty-eight on the UK charts. His first album, *Mathew and Son*, was an instant success, rising to number seven on the UK charts, and making him a pop star.

### Uncertain Fame

Stephen adopted the stage name Cat Stevens in 1966 because a friend had once remarked how his eyes resembled those of a cat. Even though his music was popular, he didn't want to be confined to one genre or style. He tried his hand at classical, soul, and other sorts of music. He also created the art for some of his later albums. Everything about him was fresh and appealing, and he became a fan favorite.

The meteoric rise to stardom left Cat Stevens reeling. He became extremely stressed. After continuous partying and travel, he fell seriously ill in 1968 at the age of only twenty years. He was hospitalized with tuberculosis, a dangerous respiratory disease. The long treatment and longer convalescence gave him time to reflect. He became interested in meditation, yoga, and different religions.

### A New Man

After his recovery, Cat Stevens came back to the musical scene with a new record company. He had written many songs about everyday situations, as well as about spiritual questions. By 1970, his music reached the United States and took that country by storm. The most popular was his iconic single "Peace Train," which cemented his reputation as a world-class singer. Some of his albums reached gold and platinum levels.

But his transformation wasn't over. While swimming in Malibu in 1976, he almost drowned. An unexpected wave saved him, and he began to think deeply about God. The next year in London, he converted to Islam and took the name Yusuf Islam. Stunning his fans and record producers, he gave up his musical career and instruments. For more than twenty years, he focused on his family and turned wholeheartedly toward philanthropy.

### Charity Begins at Home

Yusuf established several primary and secondary schools for the Muslim community in London and elsewhere. He helped create the Muslim Aid charity to provide much-needed programs in Asia, Africa, and Europe. He and his wife, Fawzia Ali, also set up the Small Kindness Charity for famine victims and orphans in Africa, and for refugee families in the Balkans, Indonesia, and Iraq. He joined the Forum Against Islamophobia and Racism to raise a voice against intolerance toward people of other faiths and races.

In 1989, a controversy arose that threatened to push Yusuf back into the media spotlight. In a television interview, he seemed to agree with a fatwa (a proclamation to Muslims ) calling for the death of writer Salman Rushdie for blasphemy. Although Yusuf later explained that his statements were misunderstood, he became a pariah in the Western world for many years. Still, his charity and music work continued. In the late 1990s, he set up his own recording studio, called Mountain of Light, where he collaborated with other Muslim singers and songwriters. He wrote and sang lyrics on Islamic themes for children, including the popular album *A Is for Allah*, in 2000.

### Return to Music

After the September 11, 2001 terrorist attacks in the United States, Muslims all over the world were harassed. Yusuf felt compelled to come back into the limelight to defend his faith. He began to speak out in the media to showcase a positive view of Islam, perform in charity concerts, and sing his popular songs, such as "Peace Train." He hoped in this way to promote unity and brotherhood among all religions.

In 2006, he released a brand-new album, *An Other Cup*. This signaled Yusuf's return to secular music after a gap of twenty-eight years. He dropped the family name Islam from his stage name and became known as only Yusuf. Over the next few years, he toured the United Kingdom, Europe, Australia, and the United States. The turnout at his concerts was overwhelming. It was as if he'd never left.

### A Musical Platform

Yusuf now uses his platform and high profile for the advancement of charitable causes such as child welfare and peace. The royalties he receives from his music support his extensive charity work. The proceeds of dedicated performances are often donated to nonprofit organizations. His 1965 song "The First Cut is the Deepest" continues to attain recognition and collect awards when sung by a variety of performers, including American country star Sheryl Crow. In 2007, he received a "Lifetime Achievement Award as a Musician and Ambassador Between Cultures" by a German record company. He was inducted into the Rock and Roll Hall of Fame in 2014 and into the Songwriters Hall of Fame in 2019.

Yusuf and his family still live in London. He sees himself as a unifying bridge between Islamic and Western culture. He creates pictures with his music, sending strong messages of sharing, understanding, and peace.

# BENAZIR BHUTTO

## FEARLESS LEADER

*Some leaders are self-made. Others, like Benazir Bhutto, have political families that propel them into the limelight. "Benazir" literally means "without equal" in Persian, and in many ways, she was exactly that. Adored by millions and hated by millions more, she walked a path that was destined to be thorny.*

### Feudal Lords

Benazir Bhutto was born in Karachi, Pakistan, on June 21, 1953. She was the eldest of four siblings, and her father's favorite. She belonged to a wealthy feudal family of Sindh, a province in the south of Pakistan. The landowners of Sindh were very conservative. They often restricted women from higher education, traveling alone, and even making their own decisions.

Benazir, however, was lucky that her family was highly educated and politically well connected. After her initial education, she went to Harvard University in the United States and, later, Oxford University in England. She studied democracy, economics, international law, and other important subjects that would help her in future political roles.

### A Political Upbringing

Benazir's father was Zulfiqar Ali Bhutto, a lawyer-turned-politician. He held various high-level government positions before becoming Pakistan's president in 1971 and prime minister in 1973. Because of her father's political connections, Benazir often had the opportunity to meet foreign dignitaries and leaders. She and her siblings grew up in an atmosphere of political wealth and influence. When her father created his own political party, she joined it. She sometimes accompanied him to international events and summits, watching and learning from him.

Everything in Benazir's life changed when she returned to Pakistan in 1977. Just a month after her return, her father's democratic rule was overthrown by a military dictator, Muhammad Zia-ul-Haq. Her father was put into prison on criminal charges and sentenced to death in 1979. Benazir and her family were also jailed on and off. She herself endured five years of imprisonment in various locations for agitating against army rule. The extreme heat, the unhygienic conditions, and the horrors of solitary confinement all affected her health deeply. Her hair fell out, her skin peeled away, and she was plagued by insects. Still, all this didn't break her resolve. She became determined to defeat Zia-ul-Haq and bring democracy back to her nation.

### Exile and Return

Finally, due to her poor health, Benazir was released in 1984 and allowed to leave Pakistan for treatment. She lived in England for two years, recovering and reorganizing the Pakistan People's Party (PPP) she had inherited from her father. She visited leaders of international importance to inform them of human rights violations in Pakistan. She was now the leader-in-exile of the PPP.

By the end of 1985, martial law was lifted in Pakistan. Benazir quickly returned to a hero's welcome. She traveled throughout the country, drawing huge crowds and making fiery speeches. She protested against Zia-ul-Haq's suspension of civil rights and incarceration of political prisoners. She was arrested again and again, but she refused to stop her work. Democracy was too important.

### Success and Failure

In 1987, Benazir got married and started a family. Many in Pakistan thought she would give up her political ambitions now that she was a wife and mother, but Benazir had no such plans. Her political activism continued, and 1988 was a year of important events. Her son was born, and her arch-enemy, Zia-ul-Haq, was killed in a plane crash. Before the year was over, elections were held, and the PPP won. As head of the party, Benazir became the new prime minister at the age of thirty-five.

The triumph was unimaginable. Benazir was now the youngest leader of a Muslim country, and more importantly, the first woman to lead a Muslim majority country in modern times. Girls everywhere rejoiced at her election. She came with an agenda of social justice and civil liberty. She removed restrictions on the press, student unions, and trade unions. She also freed women who had been imprisoned by Zia-ul-Haq's unjust laws. But she was not popular among the ruling class, and many in the PPP thought she had strayed away from her father's vision of the party. She had no political backing and was unable to pass any new laws. Her policies were ineffective, and poverty and violence increased during this time. In 1990, the president of Pakistan accused her of corruption and removed her from office.

### On Again Off Again

Benazir continued to serve in the government under the next leadership. In 1993, she was reelected as prime minister. Still, she couldn't make much difference. Violence and financial troubles plagued the nation during her rule, much like the first time. Charges of corruption continued to haunt her, and the president once again removed her from office. She decided to go back again into exile, this time to Dubai, United Arab Emirates, and lead her party from there.

In October 2007, eight years after her self-imposed exile, Benazir was pardoned of her alleged crimes. She returned to Pakistan to prepare for the next election. Hours after her arrival, an assassination attempt was made on her motorcade. She escaped, but 180 supporters were killed. Two months later, on December 27, when returning from a political rally in Rawalpindi, she was assassinated by a suicide bomber. She was fifty-four years old.

### A Complicated Legacy

Benazir Bhutto was an immensely popular leader and a champion of women's rights. However, she failed to deliver on most of the promises she had made during campaigning. She was unable to carry out her agenda for modernizing Pakistan or improving the lot of the average citizen.

Despite her position as the first female leader of a modern Muslim nation, Benazir was not universally liked. She was accused by her critics of being dishonest, corrupt, and ineffective. The violence she had tried to combat finally claimed her life, leaving a complicated legacy behind. Yet, she broke a significant barrier through her election that may have set a precedent for countless other Muslim girls and women in the future.

# RANA DAJANI

## SCIENTIST TURNED READER

*Rana Dajani learned the art, and importance, of storytelling from an early age. A biologist by profession, she never forgot her love of books. Turns out that she had an even bigger goal than genetics: reading books.*

### Young Traveler

Rana Dajani was born in 1969 in Saudi Arabia, but she grew up in the United States. Her father brought his family to Iowa in the 1970s when she was just a little girl and he was studying to be a doctor. Along with his physician duties, her father also had another important job at home: telling stories to his daughters.

Rana went to Jordan for high school and college, then got married and started a family. In 2000, she headed back to the United States with her husband and four children to obtain her PhD in molecular biology. In 2005, she returned to Jordan armed with her doctorate from the University of Iowa and a passion for genetics. She began working at the Hashemite University in Amman, teaching and researching genetics and stem cells. Among other things, her research helped create laws in Jordan related to this sort of research.

### A Reading Dilemma

When Rana returned to Jordan, she noticed something she'd never realized before. Although her home country had a very high literacy rate, most children didn't read for pleasure. This was such a marked difference from American reading habits that she couldn't help but ponder it. She decided to make this a topic of study. Her research showed that children in developing countries often lacked a love of reading because they associated it with schoolwork and curriculum. She also found how important a love of reading was for long-term success.

Rana created a philosophy called We Love Reading in 2006. She began with a simple storytime in her local mosque and established a local neighborhood library. She started reading aloud to children in different locations, wearing silly hats and making them laugh. Since then, her grassroots effort has taken on a life of its own. We Love Reading has expanded to fifty-five countries and has established more than five thousand local libraries in all sorts of neighborhoods. Volunteers all over the world are trained to become We Love Reading Ambassadors through in-person and online training. More than three thousand ambassadors carry on this important work, and more than a hundred thousand children have already been served.

### Working with Refugees

Since Rana is at heart a researcher, she wanted to back her efforts with studies and data. At the same time, she wanted to bring her philosophy of reading aloud to some of the most marginalized children in the world. She began a pilot program in 2014 at the Zaatari refugee camp in Jordan, one of the biggest camps for Syrian refugees, and conducted a study through Yale University. The results confirmed everything We Love Reading was hoping for: children who were read to showed more resilience, became better thinkers and decision makers, and wanted to study more.

Rana continued to invite more studies for her organization from academic institutions such as Harvard University. All showed the same thing: reading aloud in an entertaining way had long-term effects on children's empathy, knowledge, interests, and even behaviors. They also showed a change in adults involved as volunteer readers. They became community change makers because of their involvement.

### Support from Unexpected Sources

Rana soon began receiving attention from outside her community. UNICEF gave her a million dollars to expand her program from Zaatari to all of Jordan's refugee camps, as well as to one in Ethiopia. USAID also awarded her two million dollars for similar purposes. Rana soon recognized the need for Arabic language books, since We Love Reading advocates reading aloud to children in their native language. The organization currently offers for sale thirty-two books in Arabic. They also work with other, larger nonprofit organizations to reach more children.

Rana has received numerous accolades for her work, including five Fulbright awards and a fellowship from Harvard University. She received the King Hussein Medal of Honor in 2014 and UNESCO's King Sejong Literacy Prize in 2017. She continues to work on both her molecular biology research as well as literacy initiatives, proving to be one of the most impactful Muslim scientists of the world.

# SHARMEEN OBAID-CHINOY

## DARING FILMMAKER

*Observant, daring, angry, outspoken. These are some of the words people use to describe Sharmeen Obaid-Chinoy. She thinks of filmmaking as her own brand of activism, using stories and videos, and even animation, to lay injustices bare.*

### A Stubborn Young Girl

The eldest of six siblings, Sharmeen Obaid-Chinoy was born in Karachi, Pakistan, on November 12, 1978, into a wealthy business family. Her parents often had business guests over for dinner, and she was used to networking at dinner parties. She attended an elite, prestigious high school in Karachi, where she first honed her investigative skills. As a teen, she began to write for the local city newspapers, first opinion pieces and then investigative stories. She shocked her family and everyone else by writing about a number of controversial topics: bullying rings run by rich kids, drug habits among students, and even illegal government activities.

For the most part, Sharmeen's family was proud of her activism. At the same time, her father was very conservative, wanting her to study in the secluded environment of an all-girls' college. Sharmeen had other plans, however. She wanted to study abroad in the United States and gain important journalism skills. When her father refused to give her permission to do that, she went on a hunger strike until he relented. She attended Smith College and got a bachelor's degree in economics and government; later, she got two master's degrees from Stanford University, in communication and international policy studies.

## Exploring Documentaries

Sharmeen returned to Pakistan in 2001 to begin her activism. This was the uncertain and worrisome period right after the terrorist attacks of 9/11, and she wanted to showcase the effects of America's War on Terror. She took audio interviews of Afghan refugee children on the streets of Karachi and used them to convince the *New York Times* television production company and Smith College to fund her first documentary. She had no experience in videography, but her passion was obvious to all who met her. This film, *Terror's Children*, won her the Overseas Press Club Award.

It was the push Sharmeen needed to enter the world of filmmaking. For the next decade, she made several films using a mixture of news reporting and storytelling, often putting herself on-screen. She tackled topics such as the lack of women's rights in Saudi Arabia, the Philippines, and Afghanistan. She also focused on other marginalized groups in Sweden, Zimbabwe, and Canada. With every film she made, she learned more about the field and gained confidence in herself. The most famous film from this early period was *Reinventing the Taliban*, in which she walked among men with guns in northwestern Pakistan, asking them bold and difficult questions.

## Oscars and Emmys

By 2010, Sharmeen's filmmaking style had changed. Rather than put herself on-screen, she was focusing more on the everyday people whose stories she wanted to tell. The result was spectacular. In 2012, she made a documentary, *Saving Face*, about female victims of acid attacks in Pakistan. This earned her not only an Emmy Award, but also her first—and Pakistan's first—Oscar. In 2015, her next major documentary made even more headlines. Titled *A Girl in the River*, it tells the terrible story of honor killings from the perspective of one girl who survived. Sharmeen won her second Oscar for this timely and heart-wrenching film.

Awards are not the only outcome of Sharmeen's hard work. She aims to bring light to important but neglected social issues through her films. *A Girl in the River* led to heated discussions in Pakistan about the scourge of honor killing, finally prompting the government to enact laws against it. While she knows laws won't change people's mindsets, Sharmeen was grateful for some progress.

## Changing Minds and Hearts

Sharmeen realized that making documentaries cannot be the only role she plays in improving the conditions of marginalized people. In 2011, she created a Karachi-based studio called SOC Films, which is dedicated to bringing fiction and nonfiction storytelling to the average viewer. SOC partners with various groups to talk about important subjects, such as domestic violence, harassment, and corruption. It also showcases grassroots heroes and everyday activists from Pakistan and around the world.

Not everyone is happy with Sharmeen's work. Many Pakistanis accuse her of promoting their country's flaws to the outside world. They think her international awards are a sign that she has a political agenda, rather than a real love for her country. Sharmeen continues her activism, uncaring about these naysayers. But she does realize that many of the problems she unmasks in her films will never be eradicated from society unless people start talking about them. In 2016, she formed a mobile cinema for schools, colleges, villages, and small towns in Pakistan, using her films to jump-start important and uncomfortable conversations.

## Worldwide Activism

Finally, Sharmeen is growing into a filmmaker not just for Pakistan, but the entire world. She has built an animation studio with an ambitious goal: create movies with Muslim superheroes so that Muslim children everywhere can feel proud of their culture and heritage. She is also working on projects for a Western audience, such as an HBO documentary about college athletes, and a YouTube Original series about activists in several countries, including Kenya, Brazil, and the United States.

Sharmeen Obaid-Chinoy has certainly come a long way from the recent college graduate who didn't even know how to work a camera properly. She doesn't shy away from hard work or controversy but knows that filmmaking is the best way to improve conditions of marginalized groups, one story at a time.

# IBTIHAJ MUHAMMAD

## FASHIONABLE FENCER

*America's most popular fencer almost didn't learn fencing at all. More than a passion, this sport started as a convenience for her, something she could play while covering her body. She had no idea that decision would end up in accolades and triumph.*

### Busy Lifestyle

Ibtihaj Muhammad was born on December 4, 1985, in Maplewood, New Jersey. She is the daughter of African American Muslim parents, and sister to four siblings. Her father was a police officer, and her mother a special education teacher in the public-school system. They both were advocates of an active lifestyle, so Ibtihaj grew up always playing a sport of some kind. It was the way she and her siblings stayed in a safe environment after school and during summer vacations.

### What to Play?

Ibtihaj played a lot of different sports after school. Whether it was volleyball, softball, or tennis, she took part. She particularly liked track, but the short shorts girls wore made her uncomfortable. In elementary school, she also

began wearing a hijab and was frequently teased about it. She loved sports, but as she grew older, she found it difficult to participate because team uniforms often didn't conform with her family's idea of modesty. Searching for a sport where she could wear her hijab and cover her arms and legs, she accidentally found fencing at the age of thirteen. At her mother's advice, she joined a fencing team.

## A Competitive Nature

Ibtihaj was unsure about fencing at first. By the time she reached high school, however, she was more involved in the game and learning to compete. She became captain of her high school fencing team and led them to win two state championships. She joined a nonprofit organization called the Peter Westbrook Foundation, which helped her train with world-class coaches. Later, she won a scholarship to attend the prestigious Duke University. She continued to train and compete, becoming a Junior Olympic Champion in 2005. She was also a three-time All-American at Duke. When she graduated from Duke, she wasn't only a fencer. She had a dual bachelor's degree in international relations and African American studies, with a minor in Arabic. This was a young woman with more than sports on her mind.

## To the Olympics

Ibtihaj joined the US fencing team in 2010. She competed with her team and individually in many competitions, including the World Fencing Championships. By 2016, she was the second-best fencer in the United States and later the seventh-best in the world. From Canada to Russia and beyond, Ibtihaj represented her country as a Muslim woman wearing the hijab. Finally, she made the US Olympic team. In 2016, Ibtihaj made history by competing in the Olympics for the United States wearing a hijab. Her team won the bronze medal, making Ibtihaj the first Muslim American woman to win an Olympic medal.

## A Fashion Icon

Ibtihaj's success reminded her again of her early lack of modest but fashionable clothing for Muslim women. In 2014, she launched an online clothing company with her siblings. They called it Louella, after their grandmother. Often, as Ibtihaj makes speeches and meets with fans, she wears Louella's clothes to showcase beautiful yet modest dress. In 2019, Mattel revealed a Barbie doll in Ibtihaj's likeness, part of their Shero collection to honor women who've broken boundaries and to inspire a new generation.

## Medals for Inspiration

Ibtihaj often felt unwelcome in sports, not only as an African American but also as a Muslim. She decided to compete in the Olympics to inspire and encourage all those who felt a similar way. By breaking the barriers of elite sports, Ibtihaj feels strongly that others like her will enter competitive sports and make a name for themselves and their country. She uses her high profile as a way to bring attention to causes that are important to her. She is an ambassador for the Empower Women through Sports initiative at the US State Department. She also works closely with organizations such as Athletes for Impact and Special Olympics.

# MALALA YUSUFZAI

## THE POWER OF THE PEN

*The Swat Valley is a mountainous area in the northern region of Pakistan, well known for its phenomenal scenic views, tall mountains, and lush greenery. Then this natural beauty was marred by the Taliban. Everyone cowered against their tyranny, except for one young girl: Malala Yusufzai.*

### Trouble in Paradise

Malala Yousufzai was born on July 12, 1997 in Mingora, a city in the Swat Valley in Pakistan. Malala's father was a teacher who ran a girls' school and did other humanitarian work. Malala attended her father's school with her sisters and friends. Unfortunately, the Swat Valley was invaded by the Taliban, a fundamentalist terrorist group, in 2007. They restricted the freedom of women and girls, forcing them to stay inside their homes. They also discouraged girls' education with threats—and even with blowing up girls' schools. Malala loved going to school, but

like many others, her family was forced to leave the area. They returned when conditions eased, but only for a short time.

## The Young Activist

At a very early age, Malala became aware of how the Taliban was affecting the future of girls. Encouraged by her father, she made her first public speech at the age of eleven. It was titled "How Dare the Taliban Take Away My Basic Right to Education." When the speech was published later in the year, the British Broadcasting Service (BBC) approached her to write a blog in Urdu, about life under Taliban rule. Malala wrote the blog under the pseudonym of Gul Makai. Later, the blog entries were translated into English as well.

The Taliban were so infuriated that they bombed hundreds of girls' schools. Malala was not deterred. In a television talk show, she exposed the deteriorating conditions in the Swat Valley. This created a backlash in Pakistan and forced the Taliban to cease fire and lift restrictions on girls' education. However, girls had to observe strict rules about not going outside alone and wearing burqas.

## Fame and Laurels

Malala continued to gain recognition as an activist at home and abroad. Journalist Adam Ellick from the *New York Times* made a short documentary with Malala called *Class Dismissed: Malala's Story* and a film, *A Schoolgirl's Odyssey*. Both films were posted on the *New York Times* website. Soon, her identity as the BBC blogger became known, and she was nominated for the International Children's Peace Prize by Archbishop Desmond Tutu of South Africa. In December 2011, the Government of Pakistan created the National Peace Award for Youth and awarded it to her. The prize was later renamed the National Malala Peace Prize.

### Courage in the Face of Adversity

People started returning to their homes after the Pakistani army drove the Taliban out of the Swat Valley. However, the Taliban's presence continued to simmer underground and was to prove disastrous for Malala, now fifteen years old. On her way home from school on October 9, 2012, the Taliban stopped the bus in which she was traveling and shot her in the head. She survived miraculously, but not without having to fight for her life. She had to leave her beloved country to have surgery in Birmingham, England. She settled there with her family and, after recovering, resumed her education as well as her activism.

Malala traveled extensively and spoke on national and international forums as an inspiring teenager and an advocate of girls' education. Her focus was on women's rights and the importance of girls' education to ensure global peace and the eradication of terrorism. She established the Malala Fund in 2013 with the objective to work for every girl's right to twelve years of free, safe, quality education. The priority countries benefitting from the fund include Afghanistan, Brazil, India, Lebanon, Nigeria, Pakistan, and Turkey. As a result of her work, Malala received several awards. In 2014, she became the youngest recipient of the Nobel Peace Prize, shared with Kailash Satyarthi of India. She continues her work across the world, using her high profile to raise funds for various causes, and bring awareness to issues facing girls and women.

### Sharing Her Story

Malala's story of activism and dedication has been written by many writers, but hers is the most authentic voice. Her noteworthy books include *I Am Malala: The Girl Who Stood Up for Education and Was Shot by the Taliban* (memoir, 2013) and *Malala's Magic Pencil* (picture book, 2013). In another book, *We Are Displaced: My Journey and Stories from Refugee Girls around the*

*World* (2019), she tells the stories of refugees and other displaced individuals in addition to her own. Ban Ki-moon, Secretary-General of the United Nations, summed up Malala's vision thus: "With her courage and determination, Malala has shown what terrorists fear most: a girl with a book." In fact, Malala's own words about the power of education are as follows: "With guns you can kill terrorists, with education you can kill terrorism."

# GLOSSARY

**Al-** *(ul)*: Arabic prefix for "the"

**al-Andalus** *(ul-un-da-LUS)*: the former Islamic states in the Iberian Peninsula

**burqa** *(BUR-ka)*: an outer garment for women that covers the entire body, with a small opening for the eyes

**caliph** *(KA-lif)*: an Islamic religious ruler, regarded as a successor of the Prophet Muhammad

**caliphate** *(KA-li-FATE)*: the reign of a caliph

**emir** *(uh-MEER)*: a local Muslim chief

**fatwa** *(FUT-wa)*: a legal opinion or decree handed down by an Islamic religious leader

**hajj** *(HUJ)*: a pilgrimage to Mecca, one of the five pillars of the Islamic faith

**ibn** *(I-bin)*: Arabic for "son of"

**Shia** *(SHEE-ya)*: one of the two main branches of Islam

**Sufi** *(SOO-fee)*: a Muslim ascetic or mystic

**sultan** *(SUL-tun)*: a Muslim sovereign or king

**Sunni** *(SU-nee)*: the largest branch of Islam

# SOURCES

**Al-Ma'mun**

Al-Khalili, Jim. *The House of Wisdom: How Arabic Science Saved Ancient Knowledge and Gave Us the Renaissance.* New York: Penguin Press, 2011.

Sourdel, Dominique. "Al-Ma'mūn: Abbasid Caliph." *Encyclopedia Britannica*, 1 Jan. 2021, www.britannica.com/biography/al-Mamun.

**Al-Zahrawi**

Ramen, Fred. *Albucasis (Abu Al-Qasim Al-Zahrawi): Renowned Muslim Surgeon of the Tenth Century.* New York: The Rosen Publishing Group, 2006.

Zaimeche, Salah E. "Zahrāwī Al-. In *The Oxford Encyclopedia of Philosophy, Science, and Technology in Islam*, edited by Ibrahim Kalin. New York: Oxford University Press, 2014.

**Ibn al-Haytham**

El-Bizri, Nader. "Ibn al-Haytham" In *The Oxford Encyclopedia of Philosophy, Science, and Technology in Islam*, edited by Ibrahim Kalin. New York: Oxford University Press, 2014.

Smith, John D. "The Remarkable Ibn Al-Haytham." *The Mathematical Gazette* 76, no. 475 (1992):189–198.

**Ibn Sina**

Acar, Rahim. "Ibn Sīnā." In *The Oxford Encyclopedia of Philosophy, Science, and Technology in Islam*, edited by Ibrahim Kalin. New York: Oxford University Press, 2014.

Albert, Edoardo. *Ibn Sina: A Concise Life.* Markfield, UK: Kube Publishing, 2013.

**Saladin**

Robinson, Chase. *Islamic Civilization in Thirty Lives: The First 1,000 Years.* Berkeley:

University of California Press, 2017.

Stanley, Diane. *Saladin: Noble Prince of Islam*. New York: HarperCollins, 2002.

## Razia Sultan

Ansari, Sarah, "Islam: Early Expansion and Women: Iran to South Asia." In *Encyclopedia of Women & Islamic Cultures*, edited by Suad Joseph. www.dx.doi.org/10.1163/1872-5309_ewic_EWICCOM_0603b.

Mernissi, Fatima: *The Forgotten Queens of Islam*. Translated by Mary Jo Lakeland. Minneapolis: University of Minnesota Press,1997.

## Jalal al-Din Rumi

Iqbal, Afzal. *The Life and Work of Jalaluddin Rumi*. New York: Oxford University Press, 1999.

Robinson, Chase. *Islamic Civilization in Thirty Lives: The First 1,000 Years*. Berkeley: University of California Press, 2017.

## Ibn Battuta

Carswell, John. "Ibn Battuta (1304-1377), Arab Traveler and Writer." In *The Oxford Encyclopedia of Maritime History*, edited by John J. Hattendorf. Oxford University Press, 2007.

Dunn, Ross. *The Adventures of Ibn Battuta: A Muslim Traveler of the Fourteenth Century*. Berkeley: University of California Press, 2012.

## Zheng He

Lunde, Paul. "The Admiral Zheng He." *Saudi Aramco World* 56, no. 4 (July/August 2005):45–48. www.archive.aramcoworld.com/issue/200504/the.admiral.zheng.he.htm.

Lo, Jung-pan. "Zheng He: Chinese Explorer." *Encyclopedia Britannica*, www.britannica.com/biography/Zheng-He.

## Abdul Rahman

Austin, Allan D. *African Muslims in Antebellum America: Transatlantic Stories and Spiritual Struggles*. New York: Routledge, 1997.

Diouf, Sylviane A. *Servants of Allah: African Muslims Enslaved in the Americas.* New York: New York University Press, 1998.

## Nana Asma'u

Azuonye, Chukwuma. "Feminist or Simply Feminine? Reflections on the Works of Nana Asmā'u, a Nineteenth-Century West African Woman Poet, Intellectual, and Social Activist." *Meridians* 6, no. 2 (2006): 54–77. www.jstor.org/stable/40338702.

Boyd, Jean, and Beverly Mack. *Educating Muslim Women: The West African Legacy of Nana Asma'u, 1793–1864.* Oxford: Interface Publications and Kube Publishing, 2013.

## Naguib Mahfouz

El-Enany, Rasheed. *Naguib Mahfouz: The Pursuit of Meaning.* London: Routledge, 1993.

El Shabrawy, Charlotte. "Naguib Mahfouz: The Art of Fiction No. 129." *The Paris Review,* Issue 123 (Summer 1992). www.theparisreview.org/interviews/2062/the-art-of-fiction-no-129-naguib-mahfouz.

## Noor Inayat Khan

Atwood, Kathryn J. *Women Heroes of World War II: 26 Stories of Espionage, Sabotage, Resistance, and Rescue.* Chicago: Chicago Review Press, 2011.

Basu, Shrabani. *Spy Princess: The Life of Noor Inayat Khan.* Stroud, UK: The History Press, 2008.

## Malcolm X

Mamiya, Lawrence A. "Malcolm X: American Muslim Leader." *Encyclopedia Britannica,* www.britannica.com/biography/Malcolm-X.

Stoltman, Joan. *Malcolm X: Heroes of Black History.* New York: Gareth Stevens Publishing, 2019.

## Abdus Salam

Beall, Abigail, "Dr. Abdus Salam: The Muslim Science Genius Forgotten by History." 14 October 2019. BBC Culture. www.bbc.com/culture/article/20191014-abdus-salam-the-muslim-science-genius-forgotten-by-history.

Editors of Encyclopedia Britannica. "Abdus Salam: Pakistani Physicist." *Encyclopedia Britannica,* www.britannica.com/biography/Abdus-Salam.

**Fazlur Rahman Khan**

Khan, Yasmin Sabina. *Engineering Architecture: The Vision of Fazlur R. Khan.* New York: W. W. Norton, 2004.

Weingardt, Richard G. "Fazlur Rahman Khan: The Einstein of Structural Engineering." *Structure Magazine* 115 (February 2011):44–46.

**Ayub Khan Ommaya**

Cohn, Victor. "19-Hour Operation Saves Man's Life." *The Washington Post*, March 16, 1977. www.washingtonpost.com/archive/local/1977/03/16/19-hour-operation-saves-mans-life/dae1b6c8-f2f2-47be-b88a-e3533d6b4d53.

Kazim, Syed Faraz. "Dr. Ayub Khan Ommaya: A Luminary Neurosurgeon. *Pakistan Journal of Neurological Sciences* 4, no. 2 (April–June 2009): 90–92. www.pkjns.com/wp-content/uploads/2009/07/90.pdf.

**Farouk El-Baz**

Osama, Dr. Athar. "Profiles in Leadership (4): Dr Farouk El-Baz on Apollo Programme, Egyptian Science, and Desert Development Corridor." *Muslim Science*, July 19, 2011. www.muslim-science.com/profiles-in-leadership-series-4-dr-farouk-el-baz.

Terry, Olufemi, "Farouk El-Baz's Space Odyssey from Nasa to Star Trek," *Rocketstem*, July 9, 2019. www.rocketstem.org/2019/07/09/farouk-el-baz-space-odyssey-from-nasa-to-star-trek/on-apollo-programme-egyptian-science-and-desert-development-corridor.

**Fatima Mernissi**

Rassam, Amal, and Lisa Worthington. "Mernissi, Fatima." In *The Oxford Encyclopedia of the Islamic World. Oxford Islamic Studies Online.* www.oxfordislamicstudies.com/cite/opr/t236/e0527.

"Remembering Islamic Feminist Fatema Mernissi." *Fresh Air*, NPR, December 10, 2015. www.npr.org/2015/12/10/459223430/remembering-islamic-feminist-fatema-mernissi.

## Muhummad Yunus

https://thetech.com/2008/06/13/commencement-yunus-v128-n28

Yunus, Muhammad. *Banker to the Poor: Micro-Lending and the Battle against Poverty.*
New York: Public Affairs, 1999.

## Muhammad Ali

*Muhammed Ali Biography. Lifetime. May 23, 2006.* https://www.history.com/topics/
black-history/muhammad-ali

Myers, Walter Dean. The Greatest: Muhammad Ali. New York: Scholastic, 2001.

## Rebiya Kadeer

Basu, Arin. "I Want to Make My Fights International: Rebiya Kadeer." Radio Free Asia,
April 4, 2005. www.rfa.org/english/background/kadeer_text-20050404.html.

Kadeer, Rebiya. *Dragon Fighter: One Woman's Epic Struggle for Peace with China.*
Carlsbad, CA: Kales Press, 2011.

## Kareem Abdul-Jabbar

Abdul-Jabbar, Kareem. *Becoming Kareem: Growing Up On and Off the Court.* New York:
Little, Brown, 2017.

NBA.com Staff. "Legends Profile: Kareem Abdul-Jabbar." NBA History, August 23,
2017. www.nba.com/history/legends/profiles/kareem-abdul-jabbar.

## Shirin Ibadi

Ebadi, Shirin, and Azadeh Moaveni. *Iran Awakening: From Prison to Peace Prize: One
Woman's Struggle at the Crossroads of History.* New York: Random House, 2006.

Editors of Encyclopedia Britannica. "Shirin Ebadi: Iranian Lawyer, Author and Teacher."
*Encyclopedia Britannica,* www.britannica.com/biography/Shirin-Ebadi.

## Yusuf Islam

"Cat Stevens Yusuf Biography." Catstevens.com. www.catstevens.com/biography/.

Greene, Andy. "Yusuf Islam's Golden Years: Cat Stevens on Islam and His Return to
Music." *Rolling Stone,* January 13, 2015. www.rollingstone.com/music/music-news/
yusuf-islams-golden-years-cat-stevens-on-islam-and-his-return-to-music-241159.

**Benazir Bhutto**

Liswood, Laura A. *Women World Leaders: Fifteen Great Politicians Tell Their Stories*. New York: HarperCollins, 1996.

Naden, Corinne J. *Benazir Bhutto*. London: Marshall Cavendish, 2011.

**Rana Dajani**

"Rana Dajani: Ashoka Fellow." Ashoka.org, 2019. www.ashoka.org/en-us/fellow/rana-dajani.

Elmasry, Faiza. "Grassroots Libraries Promote Love of Reading." Voice of America, September 29, 2010. www.voanews.com/world-news/middle-east-dont-use/grassroots-libraries-promote-love-reading.

**Sharmeen Obaid-Chinoy**

Okeowo, Alexis. "An Activist Filmmaker Tackles Patriarchy in Pakistan." *The New Yorker*, April 2, 2018. www.newyorker.com/magazine/2018/04/09/an-activist-filmmaker-tackles-patriarchy-in-pakistan.

Gornall, Jonathan. "Newsmaker: Sharmeen Obaid-Chinoy." *The National*, March 3, 2016. www.thenationalnews.com/arts-culture/newsmaker-sharmeen-obaid-chinoy-1.170178.

**Ibtihaj Muhammad**

Muhammad, Ibtihaj. *Proud: Living My American Dream*. New York: Little, Brown, 2018.

Lajiness, Katie. Ibtihaj Muhammad. Minneapolis: ABDO Publishing, 2016.

**Malala Yusufzai**

Blumburg, Naomi. "Malala Yousafzai: Pakistani Activist." *Encyclopedia Britannica*, www.britannica.com/biography/Malala-Yousafzai.

Yusufzai, Malala, and Patricia McCormick. *I Am Malala: How One Girl Stood Up for Education and Changed the World*. New York: Little Brown, 2014.

# ACKNOWLEDGMENTS

We would like to thank our family and friends for their support and encouragement as we embarked on this project. We've never worked together before, so these were definitely uncharted waters for both of us. Next, a virtual hug of gratitude for our agent, Kari Sutherland, and editor, Rosemary Brosnan, who are both always ready to cheer us on no matter what.

To make sure we collected accurate information, we sought help from a number of academic sources. The advice from the following people has been invaluable in the writing of this book: Ilyse R. Morgenstein Fuerst from the Department of Religion at the University of Vermont; Kristian Peterson from the Religious Studies Department at Old Dominion University; and our incredible research assistant, Rich Heffron, at the University of Chicago. Thank you all.

Finally, a deep sense of gratitude to all the Muslim pioneers who came before us in every field, paving the way for us, and this book of our heart. We're excited to see what the future holds.

—S.F. and A.M.